THE LARGELY LITERARY LEGACY OF THE LATE LEON TOLBERT

The Largely Literary Legacy of the Late Leon Tolbert

GRANT KORNBERG
and DANIEL WALLACE
Illustrations
by STEVEN CRAGG

CROWN TRADE PAPERBACKS
NEW YORK

Text copyright © 1995 by Largely Literary Designs
Illustrations copyright © 1988 to 1994 by Steven Cragg

Published by Crown Trade Paperbacks, 201 East 50th Street, New York,
New York 10022. Member of the Crown Publishing Group.

Random House, Inc. New York, Toronto, London, Sydney, Auckland

CROWN TRADE PAPERBACKS and colophon are trademarks of
Crown Publishers, Inc.

Manufactured in the United States of America

Design by Alexander Knowlton @ BEST Design Incorporated

Library of Congress Cataloging-in-Publication Data
Kornberg, Grant.
The largely literary legacy of the late Leon Tolbert/by Grant Kornberg
and Daniel Wallace; illustrations by Steven Cragg.—1st ed.
p. cm.
1. Literature—Study and teaching (Higher)—Arizona—Humor.
2. English teachers—Arizona—Biography—Humor. I. Title.
PS3561.06615L37 1995
818'.5407—dc20 95-771
CIP
ISBN 0-517-88202-7

10 9 8 7 6 5 4 3 2 1

First Edition

It was an odd news item, to be sure, clipped from the back page of the first section of the *Times Sentinel*. Odder still was that it said so little about the runway accident's hapless victim. Certainly a college professor who manages to find his way onto an active runway deserves more attention than a spokesman from Taco Town.

But not in the *Times Sentinel.*[1]

And this is what led us to embark on our own investigation, wherein we uncovered a remarkable story—a tale that will, by turns, shock, amaze, and upset you.

Carpe diem.

---

1. *The authors, who wrote full-time for the Times Sentinel before the paper's "big downsizing of '92," have, in the past, publicly taken issue with the journal and its reporting policies. Ed.*

IN troduction

ANOTHER DAY AND AGE, Leon Tolbert's teaching techniques might have been considered progressive, experimental, or even avant-garde. In Tolbert's own day and age, however, they were considered bizarre, inane, and not worthy of a paid holiday, much less tenure. What exactly did Leon Tolbert do to elicit the wrath of an entrenched college bureaucracy which year after year not only denied him a raise but often denied that he even worked for the institution? Was Tolbert, as several of his former colleagues claim, possessed of true genius? Or was he just another fruitcake in a frayed corduroy jacket and a bad Pierre Cardin tie? Let's take a closer look.

Though he spurned convention, Leon Tolbert's approach to teaching literature was more than revolutionary. Where another professor would require a student to read, discuss, and then be tested on a text, Tolbert would go a step further.

He would require his students to *experience* a text; he wanted every reader to know the author. So, for instance, while his students were reading *The Grapes of Wrath,* Tolbert passed around a jar which, according to him, was full of dirt from Oklahoma—the very dirt and dust the Joads were fleeing on their journey west.[1] And while reading Kafka's "Metamorphosis," Tolbert brought in

---

1. *There is some evidence that the dirt actually came from Tolbert's backyard, which is full of little jar-sized holes.*

cockroaches—literally thousands of them—and let the bugs loose during his lecture, asking his class to choose the one the story's protagonist most closely resembled.

As for the style Tolbert fashioned for his lectures—what might be called the Tolbertian style—it was marked by a meandering, frivolous intelligence, lingering on inessential details, asking a great deal of the listener at times but refusing to give anything in return; it was, in short, the discourse of a friendly madman, the kind who would bury all of his money in the backyard and then forget where it was buried; the kind who would carry on long conversations with people who had dialed his number in error; a man, it must be said, exactly like Leon Tolbert.

RANDALL PIXLEY: *He was bright and articulate, no doubt about that. And his classes were certainly popular with our students. But intelligence and popularity aren't all you have to consider when a professor is up for tenure. Scholarship is an issue as well. And with Tolbert, scholarship was always a question.*

The scholarship question doggedly pursued the professor throughout the latter part of his career. Whether it was a damning comment from a colleague in a faculty meeting or a dismissive response from a journal editor to whom Tolbert had submitted an article for publication, Tolbert's professional integrity was so frequently impugned that even Tolbert himself began to think of his work as the product of an incorrigible crackpot.

That many of Tolbert's surviving lectures contain less than historically accurate information cannot be disputed; indeed, most of them contain shameless fabulations, but often it's difficult to tell the difference between matters of fact and matters of fantasy. For example, when Tolbert tells us that Faulkner's secret dream was to be a ballerina, his overwhelmingly confident, somewhat breezy style is so beguiling we *want* to believe him, and when he writes that Thoreau had a career in the family pencil business, placing erasers on the ends, assembly-line style, a part of us says, "Yes, yes!" Yet we know, at the same time, that these are the creations of a mind tethered to nothing, of an imagination gone wild, of a remedial English professor looking for salvation in the few remaining days left to him.

How should Tolbert's work be read? As the product of an individual who, at the age of fifty-six, self-destructed? Or as a diary, a self-revelation? Perhaps both of the above. For while a handful of readers may wonder why Leon Tolbert didn't simply write a novel or some other work of fiction, for most it should be clear: Tolbert, having spent the greater part of his adult life unhappily married, teaching remedial English at a second-rate state college,[2] felt, in the final analysis, that he had no life. Thus his concentration on those he felt *did*. Had he been sane, who knows what kind of sustained work he might have done?

Was Leon Tolbert, as some have anonymously suggested, a scapegoat for an educational system unable to cope with his quirky genius? Or was he, as many more have publicly sworn to under oath, the ultimate nutty professor?

---

2. *Larry Evans, dean of students at the school, has publicly taken issue with this characterization, which appeared in the October 2, 1993, issue of* Sports Illustrated. *"Dollar for dollar," Evans said, "NACC represents a tremendous value for its students, their parents, and the community at large. Please cancel my subscription after the swimsuit issue."*

There are no easy answers here. But perhaps by following Tolbert through the last semester of his life, we can come to an understanding. We can be witnesses, as it were, to his final days.

Through consultation with university records, interviews with former students and colleagues, and with the help of his mother, Stella, and his wife, Dorothea—or Widow Tolbert, as she now prefers to be called—who allowed us unrestricted access to her husband's numerous boxes of notes, quizzes, handouts, exams, unpublished manuscripts, and diaries— through all of this, a hazy picture of a man emerges.

Insane? Perhaps.

Inspired? Quite possibly.

Tenured? Never.

This is the story of Leon Tolbert's collision with literature. Consider it a cautionary tale.

Will We Ever Learn The Truth About Leon Tolbert?
by Andrew Panetta, B.A.

As close to him as I thought I had become during the three semesters we spent together, it seems I never knew just how much Leon Tolbert hated teaching college English. But, as his wife told me after the terrible accident last April, Writing was Professor Tolbert's first love. Teaching, she said, was something he did to pay the bills.

As if any of that really mattered anymore.

The Leon Tolbert I knew was a man who, after passing around a box of animal crackers at the beginning of class, would say something like, "Does everybody here know the alphabet?" or "How many fingers am I holding up?" Or sometimes, "Hey, Andy, did you forget to leave your adverbs at the door?" And of course he loved to talk.

"Did you ever hear about Benjamin Franklin's younger brother Freddy?" he would ask, and we would all shrug and say no, we hadn't, and Leon Tolbert would kick his feet up on his desk and tell us about Freddy Franklin, and when he was done we would wonder why Freddy had never been mentioned in any of the history books — especially since he had invented the retractable pencil — and Professor Tolbert would smile and say, "Why indeed?" which really got us thinking.

Why indeed?

Life is a mystery, people are a mystery, and therefore what happens to people in their lives is also quite mysterious, and this brings me to a particular March morning in Professor Tolbert's class.

"Here's a pop quiz," he said, placing a heavy manila folder on each of our desks. We opened the folders. But inside them, instead

(over)

of tests, were small mirrors. So when you looked down at your desk, what you saw was your face in a mirror in a manila folder. And professor Tolbert said, "Write about what's in front of you." That was our test—writing about our own faces. When we turned to Tolbert for an explanation and saw that he, too, was looking in a mirror and writing about it, we figured that something was the matter. It was.

A week later Professor Tolbert came to class with his tie knotted backwards and his hair nattily rumpled. He told us we al made an A-plus on the quiz."

"Even you, Panetta," he said, holding up my paper so everyone could see the big A-plus he'd scrawled across the top.

He then dropped all the papers on his desk and told everybody to write one completely correct sentence and hand it in. "Your mid-term exam!" he said.

Well, you could see he still wasn't feeling too good and that meant he would probably grade the sentences pretty tough and all, and the pressure was just so great, speaking for myself, I could barely get down "The cows grazed with an aura of contentment" before time was up.

The rest is just a sad postscript. When we returned from Easter break, we heard that Tolbert had gotten drunk one night and wandered onto an airport runway. Within minutes, he'd been struck dead by a landing plane. Was it just an accident, as the papers had reported, or had the residents of Florida merely ended their support of him?[3]

3. It appears that Mr. Panetta is alluding, erroneously, to Thomas Hardy's Tess of the D'Urbervilles, a novel he once studied under Tolbert; on the concluding page of Tess, Hardy writes, "'Justice' was done, and the President of the Immortals, (in Aeschylean phrase) had ended his sport with Tess."

The reason we want to become famous—as famous as, say, Albert Einstein—is so people can tell apocryphal stories about us when we're gone: stories that aren't necessarily true but might as well be. Everybody says, for instance, that Einstein flunked calculus in high school. This is false, of course. We, on the other hand, did flunk calculus in high school, but does anybody care? No one cares. How come?

C H A P T E R

We're not famous. We don't know anything about the space-time continuum.

Einstein even looks famous, doesn't he? Which brings us to a question it would take a mind like Einstein's to answer: Can you be famous and not look famous? We have no idea. We're neither.

—LEON TOLBERT, FROM A LECTURE
DELIVERED FEBRUARY 26, 1993

CAN YOU BE FAMOUS AND NOT LOOK FAMOUS?

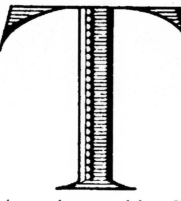

HE LAST SEMESTER of Professor Leon Tolbert's life began on January 15, 1993. Although Tolbert had been showing signs of depression since the start of the school year, his condition appeared to be worsening.[1] According to former students and colleagues, he returned from Christmas break more confused than ever.[2]

Further evidence of his deteriorating mental state surfaced at the end of January, when Tolbert began referring to himself in the first person plural. It seemed a harmless enough affectation at first, and not entirely odd. Didn't many of his colleagues do the same? "We see in the work of Melville a storyteller's love of plot. . . ." But it soon became obvious that in Tolbert's case something was different. And something *was*.

Over the next few weeks Tolbert could frequently be spotted hanging around the student center, crouched in a corner, a portable typewriter in his lap and half of a peanut butter and jelly sandwich poking from his jacket pocket. Glancing suspiciously at curious passersby, he composed dozens of lectures, some as short as a sentence in length, some as long as

---

1. *The holiday season always left Tolbert feeling empty and alone. His wife attributed this to his habit of telling everybody he could that Jesus Christ wasn't actually born on December 25, that it was originally a pagan holiday and that the early Christians merely appropriated it—and so on—the net effect being that Tolbert wasn't invited to many parties and received very few gifts.*

2. *During his first few days back on campus, he could often be seen muttering to himself and looking skyward, asking people if they'd seen his hat.*

ten pages, and many of a decidedly provocative nature.

On February 1, Tolbert's wife Dorothea returned from an afternoon of shopping to discover a garbled message on their answering machine. It was Leon, and in a voice that could best be described as hollow and distant, he was asking his wife to "give my big speckled toy to Mommy."

Dorothea shook her head, conditioned of late to Leon's bizarre messages, but thought little else of it. Later, when her husband didn't come home from school, Dorothea got worried and phoned the police. They responded by going to Tolbert's office, where they found him sleeping beneath his desk, a flask of bourbon in one pants pocket and an empty tuna fish can in the other.

We would prefer not to call attention to our intellectual shortcomings. Nonetheless we feel it's only fair to note that of all the books we've read but not entirely understood, perhaps the book we've understood least was Matthew Arnold's Culture and Anarchy, a collection of essays in which the author argues at length for the education of the "Philistines," as he refers to England's middle class, and for an end to their cold, faithless "Hebraistic" spirit.

C H A P T E R

That we purchased this book for its title, believing it to be an exposé of life on the road with the Sex Pistols, did not help matters, either.

—L.T., MARCH 3, 1993

HOUGH WE MAY very well be able to mark the day Leon Tolbert first began slipping into the murky world of madness, it would be misleading to suggest that the sickness which overtook him on that day did not have its roots in a much earlier period of his life.

Tolbert was born on September 12, 1937, to Edwin and Stella Tolbert of Pelham, New York. Edwin Tolbert had received degrees from Harvard, Yale, and Oxford, and by the time Leon was born, his father was not only a well-established translator of Greek and Roman classics but also the host of a popular literary salon known as Edwin's, where many of the great artists of the day would gather to discuss developments in their respective fields. There was, at this time, a lot of work being done on punctuation, and Leon remembered many a night when the light at Edwin's burned late indeed, as one or another literary luminary spoke with engaging eloquence on the comma and the semicolon, among other things. Edwin's wife Stella was, if anything, even more erudite than her husband, having read most of the great works, including the dictionary, parts of which she could quote verbatim. She was also a ravishing beauty and was thought to have been the inspiration for many a poem and song, including the hit "Meetcha Down at Edwin's," by Sweet Lou Lambert and the Poetasters.

This, then, was the milieu into which Leon Tolbert was born, and it was one in which he thrived. His father carried on a long correspondence with Albert Camus,[1] and Leon liked nothing better than licking the envelopes in which these letters were sent, writing in his boyhood diary, "I will contribute to the literature of this world, even if my contribution be only saliva."

No expense was spared when it came to Leon's education. He attended the finest private schools in New York City and was even tutored by Gilbert Trilby himself.

Though Edwin and Stella had high hopes for their only child, it is now clear that the pressure they brought to bear on Leon lay at the root of the many problems that would follow him throughout his later life.

Contrasting Leon's early years with those of almost any other child should be illustration enough of the well-meaning but entirely dysfunctional nature of his upbringing. While most children, for example, are merely taught to thank

---

1. *A fragment found in Tolbert's papers after his death suggests that Tolbert may have harbored some resentment over the palsy-walsy relationship his father had with Camus. The fragment, dated May 11, 1961, mockingly asks: "Are we the only ones who've noticed the eerie similarities between Albert Camus and James Dean, or—as is more often than not the case—are we the only ones who care? Take a look at this: Camus writes a novel called The Rebel, and Dean stars in a movie called Rebel Without a Cause. And this: both men smoked short, unfiltered cigarettes and let them dangle from their lips. And this: Camus was cool, brilliant, and existentially aloof, while Dean always knew that 'I want to be an actor but that isn't it. Just being . . . isn't enough. There's got be something more than just that.' Talk about existential! And, oh, there's this, too: Camus was born in 1913, Dean in 1931—identical digits, every one! And finally, both died in fiery crashes before their time."*

their parents and others for gifts or favors, Leon was required to write poems for them. His parents liked sonnets—Edwin preferred Petrarchan, Stella Shakespearean—but Leon didn't excel in either form. He did become proficient at writing limericks, however, a few of which survive to this day. This one was written when Leon was only nine and a half.

THERE ONCE WAS A BOY FEELING BLUE
WHOSE MOM BOUGHT HIM SOMETHING TO CHEW.
A HAMBURGER—NEAT!
AND AN ICE CREAM CONE—SWEET!
FROM HIS HEART HE SAYS, "MOMMA, THANK YOU!"

Leon worked hard at his writing and was quite proud of it, but his parents were never satisfied and in fact often disparaged their son's frequent use of gerund phrases. Indeed, it seemed that no matter what he wrote, it was never good enough, and Leon was distraught one morning to discover a letter his father had been writing to Camus, in which he admitted that "my son is not the genius I had hoped for, Al. His limericks don't scan well, and even his socks don't match."

When Tolbert was twelve, his parents enrolled him at the prestigious Mellon Academy, a boys' boarding school in upstate New York. Leon despised the school, "because they don't have a typing team."[2] After a lackluster semester there, Leon was abruptly called home and informed by his mother that the

---

2. In a letter to novelist Norman Mailer, dated October 12, 1949, Tolbert complained bitterly about his life at Mellon and congratulated Mailer on the wonderful reception given his first book, The Naked and the Dead. "My only regret," Leon pointed out, "is that I didn't write it myself." Though forty-five years later, in an appeal to his tenure committee, he claimed that he had.

forfeited tuition money would be taken out of his allowance bit by bit for the rest of his life. Later that same week, Leon's father installed him in the third-floor study and demanded that he write a great novel.

The best that can be said of Leon's effort is that no one ever tried harder to write a great novel. No one has tried harder to write even a good novel. And of those who have sat down and tried to write even a fair novel with some weak spots here and there and some very big problems with the main character—even among this large group of people it must be said that Leon tried hardest of them all.

He called the novel *Come Take a Nap on the Procrustean Bed, My Lovely,* and it was about a pair of mad scientists who— But that was about as far as he got. About a pair of mad scientists who—and he would get stuck, come down with a terrible case of writer's block, and spend the day cleaning out the pencil sharpener or staring out the window toward the church two blocks over. This went on for six months until his father simply gave up. "My son is not a novelist," he wrote to his golfing partner G. P. Putnam. "I am beginning to think he should go into some kind of business, as much as it hurts me to say so."

But Stella Tolbert had another idea: perhaps Leon could become a newspaper correspondent—Hemingway had been one, hadn't he? Perhaps he could parlay his love of language into a career in journalism. Though normally not disposed to agree with his mother on any matters literary, young Leon, his defenses weakened by his failure to produce a major work of fiction, felt that his mother's latest suggestion might at least be worth considering.

CHAPTER

WHY COULDN'T WE HAVE BEEN LIKE ARTHUR RIMBAUD?

HY COULDN'T WE have been like Arthur Rimbaud?" Tolbert asked his class one sunny February afternoon in 1993. "Here's a guy who revolted against every form of authority by the time he was sixteen, wrote brilliant poetry until he was twenty, and undertook some sort of 'disorientation of the senses' program for a couple of years, only to become a professional vagabond, plying his trade across Europe and North Africa.

"What a life!

"But as for us? Well, we wanted to be like Rimbaud, but we could write nothing but limericks! And that disorientation-of-the-senses bit, well, friends, we tried that too, but we could only hold out for a semester or so (we're still not quite reoriented), and now all that's left is for us to be a vagabond, but we don't want to be a vagabond, do we?

"Of course not. We want to be like William Blake. Why? Because a day doesn't go by when, on our early morning walks through this lovely college town, we don't pass a young man lying half conscious on the lawn of his fraternity house, muttering one of Blake's dicta: 'You never know what is enough until you know what is more than enough.' College, apparently, is where we learn what is enough. The young man continues to mutter, and we hear him quote Blake yet again: 'If a fool would persist in his folly, he would become wise.' The young man is merely persisting in his folly, another thing college is good for.

"And who can say but this young man might have seen angels in the trees, much as Blake did? Perhaps he fell out of a tree, chasing an angel?

"Ahhh, youth, a shame it doesn't come later in life, as Lord Asquith used to say. And a shame—but we get ahead of ourselves.

"So let's go back. About two thousand years, in fact, to the island of Lesbos, where the poet Sappho lived and wrote.

"To the west of Lesbos is a larger island called Mascus, which in Sappho's time, the seventh century B.C., was populated exclusively by males. None of the inhabitants were born there, of course, since there were no women. They came from all parts of Greece and Sicily to be with men, to live with men, and to be manly.

"And they were very manly men.

"They drank and laughed and told bawdy stories. When they spoke of women they were both disdainful and laudatory, but they came to the general conclusion that while it was difficult to live with women, it was equally difficult to live without them.

"It was at such times that the men of Mascus cast a baleful gaze toward Lesbos. What was it with those women? they wondered.

"So one morning the men of Mascus took a day trip to Lesbos. They brought bread, wine, picnic baskets, and a Frisbee. They had hoped to meet a few of the women there, for they had heard they were pretty, as indeed they turned out to be.

"But talk about cold. These women didn't seem the least bit interested in the manly men of Mascus!

"Well, one of the men, who happened to have dipped too frequently into the gourd, became somewhat angered and somewhat violent. He began writing obscenities on the walls with grape juice and knocking down statues of Aphrodite.

"Finally he was confronted by Sappho, who was very eloquent in her defense of nonviolence. Unfortunately, eloquence was not valued by this particular man of Mascus, and upon discovering a trunkful of writings on papyrus in Sappho's home, he began destroying them one by one, until he passed out and was taken away by his friends.

"And this is why so few of Sappho's poems exist today."

Sylvia Plath's first and only scheduled appearance on The Ed Sullivan Show did not go well at all, and some believe this may have contributed to the darkness one finds in much of her later work.

She was a young woman, just out of Smith, when she was contacted by CBS to see if she would like to read one of her poems on national television. Would she? You bet she would! In those days an appearance on The Ed Sullivan Show was a boon to a young poet; just look at what it had done for José Jimenez!

Anyhow, when Sylvia Plath arrived at the studio for a rehearsal things quickly went from bad to worse. As it turned out, the show's booking agent had misunderstood Mr. Sullivan's request, which was to have Robert Frost, not Sylvia Plath, appear on the program,

C H A P T E R

and when the director asked Miss Plath to read "The Road Not Taken," she pointed out that she hadn't written that poem.

"Well, what have you written?" the director asked.

"This," she said, whereupon she quietly recited a short and rather plaintive lyric.

"Fine," the director said. "That's fine. But for the show, Sylvia, we're going to want something a little more upbeat."

"Upbeat?" Plath said.

"Yes, upbeat," he said.

"I don't do upbeat," Plath said.

"Well, can you sing?" the director said. "You know, like what's her name . . . the nun."

Plath walked off the set, never to return. In her place they booked the Flying Wallendas. The rest, of course, is history.

—L.T., FEBRUARY 17, 1993

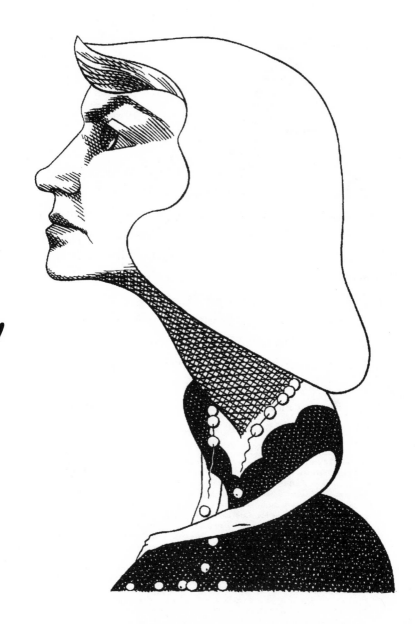

SYLVIA PLATH'S APPEARANCE ON THE ED SULLIVAN SHOW
DID NOT GO WELL AT ALL.

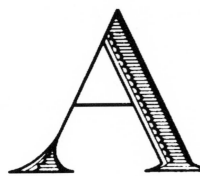ND WITH REGARD to my son," Stella Tolbert wrote to her childhood friend Winston Churchill, "I'm afraid things have not markedly improved. While Leon is clearly quite gifted, it is unclear to us how his particular gifts might be applied. We have tried everything, it seems, to no avail."[1]

It *was* clear to Stella and Edwin that Leon was no journalist, at least to judge from his first attempts at writing. As Edwin wrote in his diary, "Leon's mind lives in a strange, dark place, straddling the gulf between rationality and creativity. At any given moment, it seems, he can be either extremely logical or extremely fanciful. It is his choice. Unfortunately,

---

1. *Leon Tolbert seems never to have forgotten anyone. Churchill finds his way into one of his last lectures. He was discoursing on the Romantic poets when he told his class he had made an earthshaking discovery: in the course of his research, he had discovered that Keats suffered from premature baldness, went out without his head covered, caught pneumonia, and died. By this time, Tolbert's fantastic mental perambulations went unremarked upon by his class—a silence he understood as encouragement and, if not encouragement, complicity. He continued: "Is it our imagination, or are most great men bald? While most great women have hair—some actually have quite a lot—it does seem to us, now that we think about it, that many, if not most, of the greatest men who've ever lived were very, very bald, or seriously balding, or could at the least claim an honest, ongoing recession. Think of Socrates. Think of Hippocrates. Think of Winston Churchill. Winston Churchill, as everybody knows, was bald—perhaps not throughout his entire life, no, but of all the great things he ever did, arguably the greatest were accomplished when he had little or no hair. World War II was a bald time for Winston, as was the writing of The History of the English Speaking Peoples. We can't really imagine (and don't really care about) the younger, hirsute Churchill. Like W. C. Fields, Yul Brynner, and Mikhail Gorbachev, we prefer Sir Winston hairless. And we're pleased to note that, judging from what we see in the mirror every morning, greatness for us must be just around the corner." Tolbert had been Hippocratically bald for twenty years.*

the choice he makes is invariably the wrong one."

And yet Edwin and Stella remained undaunted. Leon was their only child; they were determined to make something of him. One night all their well-meaning yet misdirected desires came to a head when Edwin decided that Leon would make a pretty fair playwright, and Stella decided he would make a good editor.

"An *editor?*" Edwin said. "You must be joking!"

"I see nothing wrong with his being an editor, Edwin. Maxwell Perkins was an editor, and look at what—"

"I don't want my son playing handmaiden to another man's genius!"

"But editing can be very creative."

"Every editor I know is a wreck, Stella. Bitter and envious, they wish the worst on every real artist they meet, and like nothing more than carelessly rejecting work a man has spent years producing!"

"Don't put your own problems off on Leon, darling. Besides, I doubt *Outside Oslo* was rejected *carelessly.* I think Robert considered it in earnest, and he had a point: who really wants to read about Norwegian cheese farmers?"

"Forget about *my* work," Edwin said. "I want to talk about *Leon's* work. All he'd need to learn in order to begin playwriting is a little bit about form, dialogue, stage directions. Enter stage left, exit stage right, that sort of thing."

"An editor, Edwin, can be a part of so much! And Leon can still write plays, of course—if that's what he wants. But at the same time, he could shepherd the works of others to fruition, he could be the catalyst, the fire beneath the pot."

"Don't be ridiculous, Stella. I mean, let's face it, the boy's mind isn't warm enough to melt ice cream."

"Edwin!"

"Dad."

"Your father was only joshing, son."

"*Dad.*"

"I was only joshing, son."

Leon headed for the door and walked out into the night.[2]

The following evening, after dinner, Leon told his parents to stop trying to turn him into something he wasn't. "I'm obviously not a journalist," he said, "and you can forget playwriting—And editing—"

"Your father told you he was joshing," Stella Tolbert said. "Go on, Edwin, tell Leon—"

"*I was just joshing, dammit!*"

"No, you weren't," Leon said. Besides, I don't *want* to be an editor or a poet or a playwright or a novelist. I want to be something that makes the most of my God-given abilities."

"Really, now," his mother said. "You're throwing in the towel rather early, aren't you? I mean, just because you—"

"I got myself a job today," Leon interrupted. "A really *terrific* job with great pay, flexible hours, and plenty of opportunity for career advancement."

"You're learning how to pimp?" his father said.

"I'm going to be an encyclopedia salesman," Leon said.

---

2. *Where exactly he went and what exactly happened to him remain the subject of some debate; though Tolbert later told the story of leaving home that evening to countless people, he rarely told it the same way twice. In one version he was taken in by a kind old lady, in another by a pack of wild dogs. He told a former student that he stayed in a tree, living off nuts and berries; in yet another version it was squirrel meat. He had a habit of telling Dorothea that he stayed with a beautiful young woman who, in his words, "taught me everything I needed to know—years before I needed to know it."*

CHAPTER 5

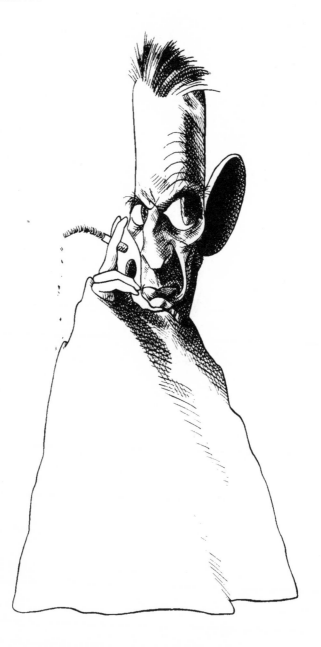

DAYS PASSED WHEN BECKETT WOULD LET NO ONE IN.

AMUEL BECKETT is one of those great writers few of us have ever actually read," Tolbert continued on that sunny February morning. "Why? Well, much of his work is, shall we say, singular? One of his plays consists of a pile of rubble, a breath, and a cry; at thirty seconds, some feel it's a bit too long. *Come and Go* has three characters and a text of 121 words—one of those rare instances in which the Monarch Notes for a work are substantially longer than the work itself. And there's *Happy Days*, a play in which Winnie is buried to her waist in a mound but still very much attached to the contents of her handbag. So there you are: three plays you already know about without having cracked a spine."

Tolbert was pacing back and forth in front of the blackboard, rubbing his hands together. "And yet," he said, "there is a great deal more out there—books by Beckett filled with lots and lots of words. What do you do? Read them?

"No. Just summarize them. For instance, in *Malone Dies*, Malone doesn't die. There you have it: an entire novel in six words.

"Beckett would be proud."

Tolbert wiped his nose with his coat sleeve and smiled. He seemed pleased with himself. "Of course, we can't mention Beckett and not mention Joyce, can we?" he said. "They were like father and son. Or maybe Joyce was more like Beckett's uncle—sometimes distant, sometimes warm, but always there, unclelike. How many of *you* have uncles?"

A few students raised their hands. Some nodded. One made the thumbs-down sign.

Tolbert cleared his throat and went on: "Well, mystery shrouds the last years of Joyce's life, my friends. It seems Beckett acted as his personal secretary toward the end—taking dictation, answering fan mail, going out for pizza, bumming money from Ford Madox Ford, et cetera. Then *Finnegans Wake* was published, and ... barely another word was heard from Joyce. Weird? *Very.* Which is why we

ask you, is it merely a coincidence that just as Joyce seemed to have dried up, Samuel Beckett became increasingly prolific? Maybe. Of course, days passed when Beckett would let no one in to disturb Joyce. 'He's thinking,' he said. 'Come back tomorrow.' And later that night the dark shadow of a man might be seen stealing through the shrubs around Joyce's cabin, his coat bulging in places, manuscript pages flying. . . ."

Tolbert thought this was a humorous image and had a good laugh over it. "Oh, my," he said to himself, "manuscript pages flying."

Suddenly he looked up, as if only just remembering there were sixty-seven students out there.

"Yes, well," he said, riffling through his notes, "as we were about to say ... What *were* we about to say? Oh, of course. We were about to say that until a few years ago the conventional wisdom among comparative literature scholars was that James Joyce invented the writing technique known as stream of consciousness. Recently, however, the scales have begun to tip in favor of Virginia Woolf, who many *now* feel was the originator of long passages with lots of subjects and objects but no periods, capital letters, semicolons, et cetera—though maybe a comma here and there. For her part, Woolf claimed not to have enjoyed Joyce's writing at all, nor did she like the man himself, for that matter, going so far as to describe him once as 'a queasy undergraduate scratching his pimples.' Now, this doesn't prove Woolf invented the stream-of-consciousness technique, of course, but it does demonstrate why we like her prose. Because James Joyce was *sort* of a queasy undergraduate, wasn't he?"

And at this point Leon Tolbert looked at all the queasy undergraduates in the room.

He drew a deep breath and continued: "As to which of them, Joyce or Woolf—or maybe even Faulkner—actually invented the stream-of-consciousness technique—well, why don't they give out patents for these things anyway, as they do for microprocessors and shower-curtain rings? You know, if writers were able to patent their styles, they might start to make some decent money. Which reminds us of T. S. Eliot. Because he worked in a bank. In London. Though he was born in Saint Louis. Yes, that's correct. T. S. Eliot was born in Saint Louis, Missouri. As to *why* he was born there, we have no idea, but we suspect it had something to do with a mix-up in the Grand Plan, the same sort of mix-up that led to Dick Sargent being cast as Darrin in the last episodes of *Bewitched*—"

The bell rang, jarring Tolbert somewhat and sending his students scurrying for the door.

As we struggle to complete this sentence, making sure all our nouns and verbs agree and that we get the spelling right, even with the big words—"geniculate," for example—and that we don't simply get lost in it—in this sentence, that is—because we let it go on too long and can't seem to find our way out, we are reminded that English was Vladimir Nabokov's second language and that he didn't begin using it on a regular basis until he moved to the United States in 1940, after which came Pale Fire, Lolita, and Pnin, and a little money and fame and censorship and, finally, Switzerland, where the great man, occasionally pausing between paragraphs (or punctuation marks) to exchange an amusing word or two with his good friend Bunny Wilson, remained until he died, and what we're getting at here is, we feel kind

C H A P T E R 6

of silly writing in this, our first language, and making it sound oddly like our third or fourth, so please forgive us, because we are not Nabokov, but then, who is?

—L.T., MARCH 26, 1993

 OOK, DAD, IT'S GOT A TERRIFIC INDEX!"

The world of door-to-door encyclopedia sales has always been a competitive one, and thus it did not surprise Edwin and Stella Tolbert that, for the fifth time in as many days, they were the target of their son's professional prospecting.

"Oh, come on," Leon said. "I've got a payment plan that's perfect for you."

"I don't believe in payment plans," Edwin Tolbert said. "I believe in cash. Payment plans, as we all know, are what drove this country to the brink twenty years ago."

"Cash is fine, also," Leon said. "In fact, with cash, I can offer you a complimentary world atlas."

"You've been here every day this week," Edwin said, trying very hard now not to lose his temper, "and every day we've informed you—*every bloody day, Leon!*—that we're not interested in purchasing an encyclopedia. We have a perfectly good encyclopedia already."

"What if I told you," Leon said, "that this entire set can be yours to enjoy, absolutely free, for thirty days!"

"What do you mean, what if you told us?" Stella said. "Since Monday you've been coming around telling us. Repeatedly.

We don't want another encyclopedia. Now, go away, Leon. Shoo, for goodness' sake. Don't you understand English?"

"Yes, Mother, I do understand English. And I understand French, as well. Do you know why? Because the encyclopedia I'm selling comes complete with a foreign language dictionary that makes looking up French words and phrases a pleasure. Do you know what *Voulez-vouz*—"

Once again the two parents shut the door in their son's face. He could certainly be annoying, couldn't he? Still, it was nice to spend so much time talking to him each day, even if the circumstances were often less than cordial. They had driven themselves mad with worry the night Leon ran away, to the extent that they'd even gone up to the attic, retrieved some of his limericks, and talked of having them published.

"He does have a certain style, doesn't he?" Edwin had said.

"A wonderful sense of rhyme," his mother said.

"Rather lyrical."

"And a pleasing voice."

"Quite ingenuous."

"Primitive, even."

"But polished."

"Yes."

"I especially like this one:

> MY MOM AND MY DAD ARE THE BEST
> MUCH BETTER THAN ALL OF THE REST
> MY MIND HAS BEEN FATTENED
> ON GREEK AND ON LATIN
> THIS IS A LIFE FULL OF ZEST!"

A

PRIL MAY BE the cruelest month, but—for Leon Tolbert, at least—March of 1993 was no walk in the park.

By the end of that month, Tolbert's desk was cluttered with notes like this:

C H A P T E R

IMPORTANT MESSAGE

TO _Professor Tolbert_

DATE _3/10/93_ TIME _3:15_ A.M. (P.M.)

M _Lance Hendrickson- asst. to Tina Brown_

OF _the New Yorker_

PHONE _212_ _555-5400_
  Area Code Number   Extension

FAX _____

TELEPHONED	X	PLEASE CALL	
CAME TO SEE YOU		RETURNED YOUR CALL	
WANTS TO SEE YOU		WILL CALL AGAIN	
WILL FAX YOU		URGENT!	

Message _Says Ms. Brown received your flowers - thanks - wants to know who you are and who gave you her home address._

Signed _____

Before Susan Faludi there was Gloria Steinem. Before Gloria Steinem there was Betty Friedan. But long before any of them there was Susan Brownell Anthony, founder of the Woman's State Temperance Society of New York and a driving force in the nineteenth-century women's rights movement. Let us hope Ms. Anthony's historical

C H A P T E R 8

stature is not diminished one iota by our government's decision, more than a decade ago, to place her splendid visage on the obverse of what was undoubtedly the most idiotic coin ever devised by the U.S. Mint—a sixteen-sided dollar the size of a quarter and just about as valuable. No, make that not even as valuable—a quarter will buy you a Tootsie Roll; a sixteen-sided dollar will only jam the machine. That they chose to feature a portrait of Susan B. Anthony on this catastrophic excuse for currency rather than a finger painting of, say, Warren G. Harding, remains one of the more inscrutable puzzles in the annals of numismatics.

—L.T., JANUARY 19, 1993

LET US HOPE MS. ANTHONY'S STATURE IS NOT DIMINISHED.

N RETROSPECT, Leon Tolbert's deci-
sion to abandon encyclopedia sales and become a college
professor seems a natural one. He was bright, well educated,
a lover of knowledge, and completely lacking in any mar-
ketable skill. Thus a career in higher education made the
most sense. At the time, however, his sudden announcement
to that effect caught his parents completely by surprise.

"You've got to be joking," Edwin said. "A professor? Of
what?" It was eight or nine in the evening, and the Tolbert
family had collected around the fireplace in their musty but
nonetheless well-appointed Pelham home.

"I don't know," Leon said. He hadn't thought about that
part. "Maybe the classics. With a specialty in eighteenth-cen-
tury Burgandian literature,[1] perhaps."

"Oh, I think Leon's just teasing us," Stella Tolbert said. "He
doesn't really want to be a college professor. Do you, Leon?"

"What's wrong with being a college professor?" Leon said.

---

1. *The literature of Burgandy.*

"Perhaps first you should graduate from high school," Stella said.

"I'm talking about *later*," Leon said.

"And when exactly is that?" his father asked. "Or, more to the point, why?"

"Don't misunderstand us," Stella said. "There's nothing wrong with teaching per se. There are many very fine teachers out there. Some of our best friends are teachers."

"In order to learn," Leon said epigrammatically, "one must be taught."

"And in order to keep the streets clean there must be trash collectors," Edwin shouted. "That doesn't mean—"

"Don't yell, dear," Stella said. "It musses your hair."

Edwin leaned forward in his chair and took a deep breath. His hair was indeed somewhat mussed. He brushed it back with his hand and looked toward the ceiling. One can only surmise what he was thinking. Perhaps he was considering his son's future—or his past. How hard he and the boy's mother had tried to find respectable work for him. How many times his son had failed. Sure, Edwin might have pondered then, each of us must live out our own special fate—but teaching! Of all things. What a waste of an occupation! Even more so than editing. What did a teacher do anyhow? Read a few books, regurgitate what he'd read in them, then expect his students to regurgitate it all right back. A rather presumptuous undertaking, if you asked him. Every teacher's dream was to have a great student, a brilliant student, so that one day he could say, "Oh, yes, I taught him. He was a student of mine." As if it really made any difference who one's teachers were. "Brilliance is as brilliance does," Edwin was known to say on more than one occasion. And he meant it.

But what about Leon? This was the first time he had thought about something he might actually want to do, something he might actually be good at! So what if it wasn't what his parents wanted—was that so bad? Maybe it was time the two of them let Leon be Leon. They could still criticize him, forever lament the day he thought of becoming a teacher, and in general do what they could to make sure their son knew they were unhappy with him, always had been, and probably always would be. It was not as though they were giving up that parental function.

"Oh, go ahead, then," his father said.

"Go *ahead?*" Stella said.

"If that's what the boy wants," Edwin said. "It's his life, right? Let him make his own mistakes."

"But you will never be welcome inside this house again," Stella said under her breath.

"Don't be ridiculous, cupcake. He can come back."

"All right, then," said Stella.

"Thank you, Father," Leon said. "Thank you, Mother. Perhaps I should compose a limerick."

"That won't be necessary," his father said. "'Thank you' is enough."

CHAPTER 9

WAS GERTRUDE STEIN A WRITER WELL YES.

EON TOLBERT sat on a granite step outside the Himmelman Humanities Center. It was raining, and the professor was soaked, yet he seemed unfazed by that fact, or by any other that didn't pertain to the matter at hand—to wit, locating a napkin on which he'd scribbled notes for today's lecture.

At Tolbert's knee was his battered leather briefcase, while scattered about his feet were its contents, a partial inventory of which included a pair of nail clippers, a Kleenex, a matchbook, a small claw hammer, two pencils whose ends had been chewed off, a nine-volt battery, a pack of Chiclets, a vial full of teeth, a box of rubber bands, a copy of *Cybernetics: or Control and Communication in the Animal and the Machine*, a squirt gun, two cubes of pool-cue chalk, a videocassette, a toothpick, a book of stamps, a dirty sock, a hairbrush, volumes VII and XI of the *Thomas Register*, a pair of ticket stubs, a can of Dr Pepper, an eight-track tape of *Superfly*, a wristwatch, a bottle opener, a harmonica, a small rubber alligator on whose belly was stamped "Souvenir of Florida," an inner tube, a bar of deodorant soap, a tube of Tester's glue, a pocket-sized appointment calendar from 1983, and a Pez dispenser shaped like Donald Duck.

"Are you okay, Professor?" It was Amy Pinkwater, one of Tolbert's star students, speaking to him from beneath an umbrella.

Tolbert looked up at her, his head cocked slightly to one side. "Oh, I'm fine," he said.

"Are you sure? It's awfully wet out here. Maybe there's something I can help you find. I'm real good at finding things." She started sifting through the mess. "What exactly are you looking for?" she said.

"I'm looking for fear," Tolbert said, "in a handful of dust."[1]

"Oh."

"Tell me this," Tolbert said, "if *i* comes before *e* except after *c*, then what comes before *c* when *c* comes before *e*?"

"Don't you want to come inside, Professor?"

"Well she was a writer," Tolbert said, suddenly remembering some of what he'd written in preparation for this morning's lecture, "a writer of all things of all the few things that she was well she was Gertrude Stein a writer well yes and Pablo said so and Alice really said so she said yes she was a writer but Papa said no he said no she was no rose was no rose was no rose.

"In one sense she made sense.

---

1. *While it appears that the allusion here is to Eliot's "The Wasteland," it's possible that Tolbert was referring, literally, to a Baggie full of dust he normally carried around in his briefcase; Pinkwater cannot recall seeing the Baggie that morning.*

"In some sense she made sense.

"So.

"She made no sense.

"She was, in a sense, Gertrude Stein. In another sense she was and in yet another she had an idea.

"Gertrude Stein had an idea of sense she had an idea an enormous idea or rather a sense of one she had something.

"Often enough they would ask what Gertrude Stein had and it was an enormous idea often enough.

"She had an enormous idea of Gertrude Stein."

Satisfied that he'd gotten it right, Tolbert slapped his knee, smiled and looked up at Amy. She was shaking her head.

"You didn't like it?" he said.

"What were you talking about?"

"My lecture," he said. "I remembered it word for word."

"You want to come inside now?" She started picking up Tolbert's belongings and stuffing them into his briefcase.

"Word for word!" he said. "I'm certain of it."

"Come on," she said, "let's get out of the rain." She escorted him inside the building.

"Word for word," Tolbert repeated several more times, shaking himself dry like a dog. *"Word for word."*

An anecdote about Frank Lloyd Wright that proves he's a genius?
How about this:

He designs a building for somebody rich and important. The building is completed, and the rich and important man moves in. But the first time it rains, a leak develops, a leak that happens to be directly over the rich man's desk. Plop, plop, plop. Fuming, Mr. Rich and Important calls Frank Lloyd Wright on the telephone.

He yells into the mouthpiece: "Wright, there's a leak in this building and it's above my desk!"

C H A P T E R *1*

To which Frank Lloyd Wright responds, "Move your desk."

—L.T., JANUARY 27, 1993

WRIGHT'S ROOF NEVER NEEDED REPAIRS.

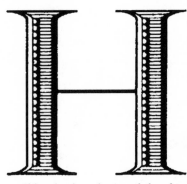AVING BEEN GIVEN his parents' blessing—or at least *not* having been shown the front door—Leon Tolbert began boning up on his lecturing technique. That evening, dressed in a sport coat and wrinkled chino slacks, he stood stiff-backed in front of the fireplace, rehearsing for the benefit of himself and his mother, who sat nearby sipping a glass of sherry.

"You, there," he said, peering into the fireplace and adjusting his tie. "You in the back. What's that you're chewing? Bubble gum? Well, I hope you brought enough for everybody. No? In that case, march yourself down here right this minute and spit that gum out in the wastebasket. That's right. Thank you, sir. Now sit down and I'll resume my discourse."

Leon's storehouse of information was vast, even when he was a youngster. He could speak freely on a variety of subjects, including literature, philosophy, music, history, poetry, and the sciences, both hard and soft. Indeed, his mind was an immense Rolodex of names and numbers, and at any given time he merely needed to flip to one that happened to interest him.

On this, his first night of lecturing, he flipped to music.

"Where was I? Oh, yes. Puccini. Did you know Puccini once described himself as a passionate hunter of women, wild duck, and libretti? But I can only assume it's to our advantage that he is best known today for his operas and not, as his father may have wished, for hunting wild duck. Call me an overeducated, stuck-up, nose-in-the-air snob, but I would rather have *Madama Butterfly* and *La Fanciulla del West* than *Puccini's Best-Loved Duck Recipes* or *The Singing Hunter: Puccini's Adventures in the Wild.* I would rather listen to *La Bohème* than read in some fish and game magazine how a hunter went duckless all weekend and thought he would go home that way until early on the last morning when he crept up to a blind and 'did a Puccini,' which might mean hitting the B above middle C, thereby momentarily rendering the ducks lakebound."

Leon straightened his tie, cleared his throat, and for a moment appeared lost in thought. He hadn't meant to go on so long about ducks.[1] But sometimes one got off the subject, didn't one? Yes, and there he was, doing just that—one minute expostulating on opera, the next minute discoursing on fowl. Perhaps he should get back to the subject at hand.

"Do you like Wagner?" he asked the fireplace.

"I despise him," Stella Tolbert said, taking a sip of her drink and shaking her head. "And your father does too. Don't you, Edwin?" She looked to the den, where her husband sat in a leather recliner, reading the London *Times.*

"Well, you shouldn't," Leon said. "You should feel sorry for Wagner. He was born without a sense of humor."

"You mean he was born without a heart," Stella said.

"You'd know all about *that,*" Edwin said loudly. "Wouldn't you, cupcake?"

"Don't be silly, Edwin. My heart's as large as your—"

---

1. Perhaps a more accurate metaphor for Leon Tolbert's mind is that it was a Rolodex that someone had dropped on the floor, scattering its cards here and there and then replacing them in a haphazard manner.

"Not only did Richard Wagner never laugh," Leon said, "he never even snickered. And when he made love to his wife, he did so fully clothed, standing up in a closet, while he forced her to read Plato to herself, backwards."

"Oh, my," said Stella. "Sounds like it could be—"

"Enough!" Edwin called out.

"His children grew up trying to make him smile," Leon said. "They told him some of the funniest jokes in the world, and still they were unable to make him smile. They told him the very famous joke about a man going into a café and ordering a cup of coffee without cream. Soon the waitress came back and told him they were out of cream, would he mind taking his coffee without milk?"

Leon's mother threw back her head in laughter, and Leon paused for a moment, wondering what had happened. He'd meant to say something trenchant about the Ring Cycle, and had somehow gotten carried away with the popular conception of Wagner as a humorless man. Why had he digressed so? He looked into the fireplace. What kind of teacher are you? he wondered. Harvard material? Princeton, perhaps? How about Yale?

Try Northern Arizona Community College, the embers must have said.

CHAPTER 11

MID-TERM EXAM

1. Imagine what it would be like to go out to dinner and discover that sitting at the table next to you, well within eavesdropping range, are Ernest Hemingway, Oscar Wilde, Gertrude Stein, and Virginia Woolf. What are they talking about? What are they eating? How are they dressed? Who slaps whom first and why? (5 POINTS)

2. Hemingway blew his brains out with a shotgun; Woolf committed suicide by drowning. How would you kill yourself if you were a famous writer? Be explicit. (7 POINTS)

3. Who's the funnier novelist: Melville or Hawthorne? How many jokes can you find in *The Scarlet Letter*? Should we make fun of Billy Budd's speech impediment? Ahab's wooden leg? In *Moby Dick*, who gets the most laughs? (4.21 POINTS)

4. You're playing strip poker with some of the twentieth century's most notorious writers. D. H. Lawrence is there, and so are Anaïs Nin and James Joyce. Suddenly Henry Miller jumps up from the table and draws his gun. Who is he pointing it at? Why? Do you stay put or head for the door? Who's the tall bearded man in the corner? (11 POINTS)

5. If *Absalom, Absalom!* had been written on a computer, would Faulkner's sentences have been longer or shorter? Comment same if the book had been written with a rock and chisel. Fingernail polish? Bread crumbs? If Faulkner had had only napkins and bacon grease to work with, what sort of books would he have written? (16 POINTS)

6. Pretend you're a verb. (9 POINTS)

7. Robert Frost once said that writing poetry that doesn't rhyme is like "playing tennis without a net." Explain what he meant. Who said that writing modern drama without an NEA grant was like "playing soccer without a goalie?" (8 POINTS)

8. If poets were basketball players, who would be most likely to take it to the hole? Shoot jumpers? Who would be your defensive stopper? (3 POINTS)

Our Rod Serling imitation is coming along. We do him at parties, at work, for friends and acquaintances we meet on the street. We do him all the time. He's getting better, and everybody seems impressed.

Where a lot of Rod Serling imitations go wrong is in the face: no one works to get the face down. Or the stance. A lot of people think when you get the voice down you've got Rod Serling, but nothing could be further from the truth. When you get the voice down, what you've got is the voice; what you don't have is the man. We've got the man. We talk Rod Serling, we walk Rod Serling, we eat, sleep, dress, and chain-smoke Rod Serling, we're even thinking of having our name legally changed to Rod Serling.

C H A P T E R *1*

Of course we do Rod Serling doing The Twilight Zone. Kid stuff. Anybody can do Rod Serling doing The Twilight Zone.

But how many people do Rod Serling ordering a martini at a crowded bar? Or talking to his wife on the phone? Or trying to explain to a film crew the difference between a bagel and a doughnut?

We do all of that. In fact, we frequently do Rod Serling better than Rod Serling did. It's as if we've fallen through some strange hole in time, or into a parallel universe, as if what we once thought of as a game, as a harmless impersonation, has taken over our lives and transformed us into hideous caricatures of . . .

Doo-dee doo-doo, doo-dee doo-doo.

—L.T., APRIL 1, 1993

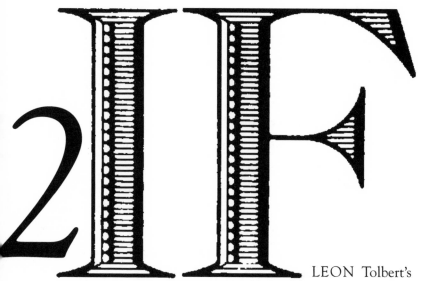

LEON Tolbert's father, Edwin, is remembered for anything today, it for his theory of osmotics (taken from the Greek *osmosis*). Osmotics is a theory of learning based on the belief that a person has the ability to learn simply by being in the presence of great intelligence. A person who is taught according to the principles of osmotics doesn't have to study or even read; he merely has to be "attentive to the radiating impulses of genius" emanating from the "passive teacher." Edwin spent a great part of his life perfecting the theory of osmotics, and another great part of it trying to find a publisher interested in printing it. Finally he paid for the publication of a pamphlet that summarized his ideas, many copies of which he sent to his famous friends. But despite his contacts in the world of learning, as far as is known only one person was actually taught osmotically. That person was Leon Tolbert.

From the day he was born, Leon was taught by a succession of passive instructors. The list was long and impressive. George Orwell, Dorothy Parker, Jean-Paul Sartre, and even Rod Serling[1] were among those Leon watched and sat with, sometimes for hours at a time, attentive to the radiating impulses of genius emanating from them. Afterward, his father would test him on what he'd learned. When Sartre visited the Tolbert residence, had tea and cookies, and spoke of little more than how unbearable Paris was in August, Edwin asked him whether existence preceded essence, or essence existence. The subject had never come up, and yet Leon's answer—"Don't be silly, Dad: existence!"—convinced the elder Tolbert that osmotics was possible.

Thus, when Leon decided he wanted to become a teacher, Edwin was certain that the best way to learn how to become one was through his osmotic method.

"Simply go down to the university and audit a couple of classes. Of course, you'd actually have to see the teacher teaching, now, wouldn't you? I can't imagine they'd simply let you *be* with them. It might still work, however, a form of secondary osmosis in which you observe the style, actions, inflections of the subject, leading to—"

---

1. Though best known as the host of the popular Twilight Zone television series, Rod Serling was also a gifted playwright and thinker, able to discourse at length on almost any subject, from poetics to social engineering. He was said to have made quite an impression on the teenage Tolbert, who idolized him. In fact, Leon preferred being osmotically taught by Serling over anybody else, even Sartre, whose wandering eye gave him the heebie-jeebies. While he taught Leon, Serling liked to play a rousing game of Ping-Pong, after which he might say, "So what about that 'Ode on a Grecian Urn'?" To which Leon would respond, "Love it!"

"Excuse me, Edwin," Stella said, "but have you seen my shoe? My left shoe, actually. I had them both here, but now I can only seem to come up with the right one. Odd, isn't it? Or should I say, 'even,' it being the right shoe I've found, that is, and the left one I seem to be missing? I was making a joke, Edwin. . . . Edwin? Are you paying attention?"

"Of course I am. And you're right. That is odd. But I was talking to Leon about osmotics."

"I know, dear. And I was talking about my left shoe."

"Didn't you put it in the oven, Mother?"

"In the oven?" Edwin said.

"Of course! I stepped in that puddle at the stoop and put my shoe in the oven to dry. Thank you for reminding me, Leon. Continue, Edwin."

"Continue? With what?"

"With what indeed?" Stella said. "Shall we go, Leon?"

"Let's," Leon said. "I'll get your shoe."

CHAPTER

"THE ALGONQUIN HOTEL in New York, SHAKESPEARE AND COMPANY in Paris, 3 HARRY'S BAR in Venice.

If those walls could talk!"

At this point Professor Tolbert bent down to tie his shoelace, and as he did so, he noticed something that both startled and delighted him: there, in the far corner beneath his desk, was the mysterious vanishing napkin, the one on which he'd written his lecture notes. Why, for crying out loud, it had been here in his classroom the entire time! And to think he'd been under the impression that he'd lost it!

Tolbert grabbed the napkin, stuffed it in his jacket pocket, stood back up, and continued.

"Have any of you heard of the White Horse Tavern?" he asked his class. "In Greenwich Village? In the city of New York?" Tolbert waited several seconds for a response, but none came. This was not unusual. His students rarely responded, but of course that was why they were students, he surmised, because they were incapable of thinking for themselves. Teachers think for themselves, writers think for themselves, philosophers think for themselves, why, even editors think for themselves—every once in a while, at least—but students, well, they merely regurgitate— And at that moment Tolbert came face to face with the miserable truth, the same miserable truth he'd come face to face with each morning since he started teaching more than twenty years ago: his parents had been right! His profession *was* a waste. He'd have been better off if he'd stuck to selling encyclopedias. At least that way his mother would have let him come back home.

The possibility that we are the illegitimate offspring of F. Scott Fitzgerald and a day maid at the Sherry Netherland Hotel in New York has occurred to us, but we've since discarded the idea as little more than a cheap publicity stunt, the product of our own unquenchable greed. The only chapters missing from an otherwise supremely tumultuous life, however, are two or three kids Fitzgerald never knew about suddenly showing up at his door. Not that Fitzgerald was promiscuous, but, come on, who are we trying to fool? It

C H A P T E R 14

could have happened! But what truly mystifies us is how he drank so much and wrote so well. Allegedly at the same time. Most people we know have to specialize: our friends who specialize in drinking, for instance, are not much good at writing, and vice versa. But maybe it's just the times we live in. These days it seems less de rigueur for writers to kill themselves with drugs and alcohol—a trend we find refreshing. Though not necessarily conducive, we hope, to someone's writing Daisy, the Sequel.

—L.T., MARCH 11, 1993

HE FIRST class Leon attended was taught by a tall man in a dark suit who walked back and forth in front of the blackboard and raised his right hand when he wished to make a big point. Leon liked this style, and sought to incorporate it into his own. In his mind he saw himself walking back and forth in front of a blackboard, making a big point by raising his right hand. But when he returned home that afternoon and tried it himself, he found he couldn't do it: the mannerisms did not feel natural to him. He literally could not walk and talk at the same time. As Edwin and Stella exchanged puzzled stares, Leon broke down, convinced he would never become a teacher.

"The osmotic method," Edwin said reassuringly, "even when it's secondary osmosis, takes time. Be patient, son. And anyhow, we may be moving too fast here. Perhaps this professor's technique wasn't the best fit for you. Perhaps you should attempt this secondary osmoticization through some-one else."

The next day Leon returned to the university, and this time he attended a lecture given by a different professor. This other professor sat behind a large desk. His arms rested on the desktop and didn't move. As he spoke, his eyes slowly panned the classroom while the rest of him remained motionless. This professor seemed to be admired by the students, so Leon attempted to mimic his style that evening at home.

"I'm fond of Ralph Waldo Emerson," Leon began, fighting to keep his hands still in front of him. "Believe it or not, he's a lot like me, or rather I'm a lot like him. The first uncanny resemblance is this: Ralph Waldo Emerson was not that great a student, and *neither am I.* Of course the resemblance doesn't stop there. For example, Ralph Waldo Emerson quit his first job after a very short period of time, *and so did I!* Hard to believe the similarities, isn't it? Furthermore, Ralph Waldo Emerson's transcendentalist philosophy, which relies on intu-ition as the only way to accurately comprehend reality, is, well, it's sort of like my philosophy . . . I think . . . though I always like to ask my mother her opinion first."

"And that's why you're so smart," Stella Tolbert said, pat-ting her son's shoulder.

"I can't keep my stupid hands still!" Leon shouted. "They just keep . . . moving!"

Indeed, as he sat at the dining room table, his father in a folding chair across the room, pretending to be his student, Leon's hands jerked this way and that. After seconds of almost perfect stillness, he would suddenly have to scratch his nose.

"Perhaps if you relaxed," Edwin suggested.

"Yes," his mother said. "Talk to us."

"About what?"

"I don't know," Edwin said. "Try Swift."

"Swift," Leon said, and cleared his throat. "Jonathan Swift. In 1689, when he was twenty-two years of age, Jonathan Swift became a secretary. He took dictation, read the mail, and no doubt would have answered the telephone had it been invented at the time. You see, in 1689 it was not uncommon for young men to become secretaries to older, more distinguished gentlemen; sometimes, as in the case of Swift, it was the first step in a series of steps toward a more professional career. And though this has absolutely nothing to do with Jonathan Swift, one has to wonder why the same isn't so today for those young ladies who begin, and sometimes end, their careers as secretaries. Indeed the nature of the job seems to have changed with the sex, which, come to think of it, does have something to do with Swift, as he would have railed against the injustice of it all, perhaps writing another 'Modest Proposal,' this time encouraging secretaries to eat their employers. Though we doubt many would take him up on it: working for those guys is bad enough; having to digest them would be just awful."

Edwin smiled tentatively, and Stella, for no particular reason, clapped. There was nothing, really, to clap about: throughout the entire speech Leon's hands couldn't keep still; they were, in his father's words, "like hairless little rodents, scuttling across the table in front of him."

Leon was crestfallen.

"Keeping still is not necessarily the highest virtue of a good professor," his father said. "I've known lots of professors whose hands moved. Why don't you try to speak moving just one of your hands?"

"Speak about what? I'm running out of—"

"Elizabeth Barrett Browning," Stella suggested.

"I've never read—"

"Oh, for God's sake, Leon. It doesn't matter what you've read!" Edwin was being particularly fatherly now. "When you're a professor it's only important that you *seem* to have read. Now go ahead and *seem*."

"Okay, then," Leon said. "Elizabeth Barrett Browning, besides being a great poet, knew practically everybody. She knew Robert Browning, of course, and she married him. But there were also a lot of people she knew and didn't marry. Ruskin, Carlyle, Tennyson, Thackeray, Rossetti, Hawthorne, and *many*  *other famous people*. She knew all of them. And what do you think these famous people talked about when they got together? Poetry? Nope. The meaning of life? Hardly. What these famous people talked about was who among them was the *most* famous. They would argue endlessly about it while Elizabeth Barrett Browning listened, silent; she was not as interested as they were in fame. As Tennyson grumbled about how he was poet laureate, which meant that *he* should be most famous, Elizabeth Barrett Browning quietly composed some of the loveliest poems I've ever read."

"I thought that was very nice," Stella said. "I think her poems are lovely, too. And I've actually read several of them."

"Did you see his hands?" Edwin asked her. "They looked as if they had a mind of their own. Both of them. It's weird."

But Leon wouldn't stop now. Hands or no hands, he would teach!

"Let me tell you about the Brontë sisters," he said. "The Brontë sisters are to English literature what the Andrews  Sisters are to American music. Not that the Brontë sisters didn't give singing a try. They did, or rather they thought about it, or rather *Charlotte* thought about it: singing with her sisters was always Charlotte's dream. But Emily and Anne *never* went along. Not if it was something Charlotte wanted, oh, no. Emily and Anne this, and Emily and Anne that, but Charlotte? Never. Singing? Forget it! We're too busy to sing et cetera and so on. We're *writing*. La-di-da. Well, I can do that too, Charlotte said. And she went off and wrote *Jane Eyre*, just to tick them off. La-di-da."

Leon stopped to breathe, and was about to begin again— "Jules Verne," he screamed—when Edwin held up his own hands and shook his head.

"Now, now, Leon," he said. "We're getting ahead of ourselves here a bit. Relax. Remember, Rome wasn't built in a day. For heaven's sake, even Pittsburgh took several weeks. Let's not rush."

"Patience is a virtue," Stella said.

"So is originality," Edwin said, cutting his eyes at her. "At any rate, I think I sense the problem. While your goal, obviously, is to one day become a professor at a university—and a fine one you'll be, son, an extraordinary teacher, indeed!—that time hasn't yet come. That time, in fact, is some way off. We need to remember that the grandest house also has a mighty foundation."

"Now, *that's* original," Stella said. "Last time I heard it, three wise men came to Bethlehem."

"What are you getting at, Dad?"

"We need to better understand the fundamentals. These college professors, walking and talking, sitting and talking, et cetera, they make it look it so easy. The truth is, they've practiced their mannerisms for years. Much of the time they've had to work their way up through the ranks as well. And I think that's what you'll need to do."

"You mean—"

"That's right. You'll learn technique from the ground up."

"You mean—"

"An elementary school teacher."

"You mean—"

"*I mean,*" Edwin said, "that tomorrow you will attend class with a dozen or so sixth graders."

"Sixth graders?" Leon said. "*Sixth graders?*"

"The daughter of a dear friend of mine teaches sixth grade at Johnson Elementary. I'll call him immediately. I'm sure he'll—"

"Father," Leon said, "I don't think I can do that. I mean, I'm almost twenty years old."

"Nonsense! You want to become a teacher, don't you?"

"Yes, but—"

"Then you must be willing to make the necessary sacrifices. Dreams don't just happen, son. You have to make them happen!"

"Another zinger," Stella said. "From God's lips to our ears."

"Do I have to, Father?"

"Or move out, son."

"Then I suppose I will," Leon said. "Go back to sixth grade, that is."

Perhaps Leon Tolbert would have been more willing to go if he'd known that he would meet his wife in that classroom the following morning. On the other hand, perhaps he'd have gone hunting for an apartment.

CHAPTER 15

The Literary Olympics:

WHAT BEGAN one hundred twenty-seven years ago as a single-event competition between Walt Whitman and Thomas Carlyle has blossomed into a literary extravaganza that annually plays host to more than a thousand distinguished participants from around the world. We're talking, of course, about the Literary Olympics, held each September in lovely Uniondale, Ohio.

Who can forget the 1937 Olympics, with Winston Churchill's dazzling victory over Lady Astor in the Inadvertently Self-Reflexive Three-Line Insult:

Astor: You, Mr. Churchill, are a drunk!

Churchill: And you, Lady Astor, are ugly!

Astor: But tomorrow morning, Mr. Churchill, when I arise, I shall still be ugly, while you, I'm afraid, will have sobered up. Excuse me, that's not what I meant. I meant that tomorrow morning, when you arise—you, Mr. Churchill, when *you* arise—you will be sober, while I—when you arise, that is—well, I, Lady Astor, shall still be ugly. No, no, I take that back! Oh, goodness, look what you've got me saying, Mr. Churchill!

A Uniondale Tradition

A gold medal performance.

And just as memorable were the 1922 Olympics, where semantic mayhem ensued when Gertrude Stein and T. S. Eliot were pitted against James Joyce and Ezra Pound in the Tag Team Declamation and Debate finals.

"Were there somewhere there were there were somewhere," Stein spat out, "there we sat we were there where were we there or here where we were—"

"Yet those teensy-weensy tickety-wicketies," Joyce broke in, "chanced to pluck their weary, leery—"

"Crete, with dizzy eyes, cried $\Omega\Sigma\phi$," Pound interjected, "GLASS doKtors! dead CEREMONIES!"

"Down the streets," Eliot barked, "Ill-conceived conceits, unremarkable retreats, rotting parsley and ashen beets."

That event, of course, came to a draw, despite Stein's last-minute attempt to perform a Triple Icepick: a thirty-three-word sentence using only one verb.

Sadly, she fell asleep just two syllables shy of victory.

In the spirit of honesty we would like to admit, for the first time anywhere, that, though we began Thomas Pynchon's magnificent novel Gravity's Rainbow (and have since found many occasions on which to express an opinion of it) we did not exactly finish that book. The same can be said of James Joyce's opus Finnegans Wake, which we toted around campus for six semesters, talked loudly about in smoke-filled dorm rooms, and in fact based our honors-winning master's thesis on before finally conceding to ourselves that we were never going to finish all 900 pages until we got through the first 900 words. So what does any of this have to do with John Steinbeck? Well, it has a lot to do with John Steinbeck, because John Steinbeck is one of the few authors we talk about whom we've

C H A P T E R 1

ever actually read. That's right. While we never came close to fin-ishing Finnegans Wake or Gravity's Rainbow, we devoured every last syllable of both Cannery Row and Of Mice and Men. And as long as we're at it, we might as well support Auden on a point he made just before delivering a lecture on Don Quixote: he said he'd never finished the novel and doubted anyone in his audience had, either. Well, believe it or not, we had the good fortune to be in that audience, and naturally we roared our approval. Of Don Quixote, that is. We'd never even heard of Auden.

—L.T., MARCH 16, 1993

ONE OF THE FEW AUTHORS WE TALK ABOUT

WHOM WE'VE EVER ACTUALLY READ.

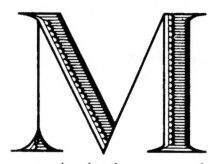ISS Dorothea Insko's sixth graders sat at their small brown desks so still Leon might have thought they had been frozen there by the magical will of Miss Insko herself. They were certainly a handsome group of youngsters, boys and girls in pink and blue with their hands clasped together in front of them, not speaking, their eyes focused straight ahead on the blackboard, which was actually green, where their teacher was writing the name Mark Twain. Leon sat in the back of the class, hands folded in front of him, eyes forward: a giant impersonating a dwarf. He was much taller than his fellow classmates, of course, and wider and, at the age of nineteen, more than eight years older. That being said, he still felt, as only Leon Tolbert could, insecure, even sort of *behind*: prior to the start of class he'd overheard a couple of the boys talking, and he found it hard to follow them; the slang they used was unfamiliar to him. He tried his best to feel superior—How many of these kids know what "parthenogenesis" means? he remembered thinking—but for all his inculcated snobbery he could not, and by the time he took his seat in the back of the class, he felt smaller than the smallest kid there, who happened to be Tim Kreider, four feet eight inches tall and sixty-seven pounds.

But Leon wasn't there to feel one way or another, he reminded himself; he was there to learn. He was there to learn some fundamental teaching techniques from a woman only a few years older than he was, and off of whose ankles he couldn't keep his eyes. They were thin and white and somewhat bony—fine, he might have thought to himself. As she stretched to write "Samuel Langhorne Clemens" above "Mark Twain," he was able to see a small part of the pink pad of her heel slipping out of her low-cut leather shoe, and he wondered if any of the other boys had noticed it. Probably not: they had already picked up their pencils and were scribbling little notes. Leon promptly did the same, although his notes were somewhat different from those of his classmates: "Good posture. Back to class as she writes, arm bent at precise ninety-degree angle. Chalk held between thumb and forefinger with authority, almost as though she were teaching it to heel. Her cursive writing is very neat."

Leon liked her style. Better still, he was able to osmotically imbibe it. As he watched, he felt the experience and knowledge of this young sixth-grade teacher enter and become a part of him. For the first time he was certain he too could become a teacher. And she hadn't even turned around yet.

When she did, something in Leon's throat tightened up, as though he'd suddenly realized where he was and by whom he was surrounded. Miss Insko had small brown eyes and dark caterpillarlike eyebrows that stretched across her forehead. She didn't smile so much as press her lips firmly together into a thin red slit, which made her cheeks bulge out like a chipmunk's. Her hair was curled into tight little knots, and her neck was thin and tense.

Oh, my goodness, Leon thought: here before him was a *woman*. Regardless of the story he told of his week away from home, Leon had not had that much experience with women. In fact, he had met only a few of them in his entire life. He had fond memories of certain women whose hands he'd shaken. He remembered with a special relish certain female friends of his parents who pecked him on the cheek, some of them well into his teen years.[1] There is evidence to support the assertion that Leon was a virgin at the time, but there is certainly no evidence to suggest that he wasn't. In a letter to the jazz pianist Oscar Peterson, Edwin Tolbert wonders if his son "perhaps doesn't require the company of women," but he later abandoned that theory when he noticed that Leon "blushed every time Dorothy Parker came into the room. Or left it, for that matter."

"Now, tell me," Miss Dorothea Insko said, "how many people's names have I written on the blackboard? Jeffrey?"

"Two," said the confident brown-haired boy in the front row.

"Wrong," Miss Insko said.

"You—"

"Wrong, Jeffrey. Wrong, wrong, wrong. Had I asked how many *names* are on the board, you would have been correct. But I asked how many *people's* names. You should listen more closely."

"Still . . ." Jeffrey said.

"Which is what I wish your mouth would be," she said. "Still."

Touché! Leon thought, noting the gentle firmness of her delivery. "She takes no guff," he wrote.[2]

"Now," she said again. "Anybody? How many different

---

1. *Gypsy Rose Lee was a longtime favorite of Leon's.*
2. *In his career as a teacher, guff was something that Tolbert tried not to take either.*

people's names have I written here?"

As there were no takers, Leon hesitantly raised his right hand.

"Yes," Miss Insko said, as if he were just another student. "Leon?"

"Though two names are written there," Leon offered, "one person claims both. Mark Twain was the pseudonym of Samuel Langhorne Clemens."

"Very good, Leon. You get a gold star for that answer." She walked over to him and affixed a small gold star to his forehead.

A gold star! Leon thought. What a grand idea! He too would offer gold stars to his students when they gave the correct answer.[3]

But another question had been answered at that exact moment, a question his heart had been asking, silently, for many years: Where is my true love? How will I find her? What does she look like?

Her name is Miss Dorothea Insko, his heart said. She teaches the sixth grade. And she looks like a cross between Humphrey Bogart and Marlene Dietrich.

---

3. *Though he began his teaching career offering gold stars to his students, Tolbert soon tired of it; to a teacher paid just above minimum wage, the cost of gold stars, though small, was prohibitive. In his later years, he would bring a pocketful of pebbles from his walkway, and when a student answered a question correctly, he would toss him one.*

"New Yorker."

"Tina Brown, please."

C H A P T E R 1

"May I tell her who's calling?"

"John Updike."

"One moment."

"Thank you."

"Mr. Updike, Ms. Brown is in a meeting. Would you like to speak to her assistant, Lance?"

"I suppose."

"One moment. I'll connect you."

"Mr. Updike?"

"Lance?"

"No, it's still me. Lance is out to lunch. Would you care to leave a message?"

"Yes, I would. But for Tina. Tell her— *I'm* sorry, I didn't get your name."

"Jasmine."

"Jasmine. What a pretty name. I once had a sister named Jasmine. We lost her in a boating accident."

"That's unfortunate. Your message?"

"Quite. Anyhow, tell Tina—pardon me, Jasmine, my secretary's trying to signal—what's that? One moment, Jasmine, I've got J. D. Salinger trying to buzz in on the other line."

"Perhaps you'd like to call—"

"Why don't you just patch me through to Tina, okay? I promise I'll keep it short."

"You're not John Updike. I know that. You're Leon Tolbert. And Lance said—"

"He returned my manuscript?"

"Yes. And he also said not to put you through to Tina. And he also wanted to know who gave you Tina's—"

"I thought Lance was at lunch."

"He was."

"When? Yesterday?"

"Hey, look Mr. Tolbert or John Updike or Whoever-You-Are, I've got a million calls coming through, and I'm going to get fired if I sit here talking to you all afternoon, so I've got to hang up, right now, okay?"

"Anything you say, Jasmine."

"So long."

"Bye."

"I thought you were hanging up."

"I was. Or rather, I am. As soon as you do."

"Well, that's now."

"*Adios.*"

"You're *not* hanging up."

"Wrong. I *am* hanging up. At least I'm in the preparatory stages of hanging up. The actual placement of the handset on the cradle will come after I've ascertained that *you've* hung up."

"But I can't hang up until you hang up! You called me, remember? It won't disconnect until you've hung up, so hang up now, *all right?*"

"Jasmine."

"Now!"

"I miss my sister so much."

"I don't believe you had a sister named Jasmine."

"She was so pretty. I mean, until the propeller—but you don't want to—"

"Lance says you're a pathological liar."

"Jasmine and I used to write short stories together. Tag-team style. I'd write the introduction, she'd write the conflict, I'd write the exposition, she'd write the climax, I'd write the . . . Jasmine? Are you still there, Jasmine?"

"No, I've hung up."

"You're upset with me, aren't you?"

"I think you're a nut."

"But you don't *really* think that. You simply *think* you think that because of something Lance told you. Can I tell you something about Lance?"

"No, you cannot!"

"He was a student of mine at Cordell Union."

"I'm hanging up, Mr. Tolbert."

"But we're just getting to be friends."

"Good-bye."

"See you, Jasmine."

"Ciao."

Philip Marlowe couldn't write, and that's why Raymond Chandler was born. Or maybe it was the other way around and for different reasons, but frankly, it's difficult keeping them apart. For instance, Chandler wrote, "I was neat, clean, shaved and sober, and I didn't care who knew it," but Marlowe actually said it: Chandler never would have said something like that. Chandler was a writer, for goodness' sake. He was educated in England and was, in fact, a very literary kind of guy, so literary he knew he was writing literature before anybody else did. Some people still aren't

C H A P T E R

18

quite sure, but what do they know? His books are great and so are their titles: The Big Sleep; Farewell, My Lovely; The Long Goodbye—*just to name a few. See how they all refer obliquely, poetically, to death? Chandler knew what he was doing. He knew you didn't have to write about some fragile, tea-sipping type of man to write something worth reading. People called his stuff hard-boiled because the private dick is such a tough lug, but don't believe it. Beneath all those scars, cuts, and contusions is a wildly sensitive heart. Just don't get in his way, let him do his job: he's the good guys.*

—L.T., FEBRUARY 26, 1993

"I BEG YOUR PARDON?" HEMINGWAY SAID.

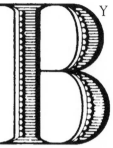Y THE END of his first class with Miss Dorothea Insko, Leon Tolbert had accumulated fifteen gold stars, fourteen more than the rest of the class put together. "Things got out of hand somehow," the widow Tolbert remembers now, "and after a while he just seemed like another sixth grader. A bright sixth grader, and exceptionally large, but, all in all, not that much different."

Certainly his day in class did wonders for his self-confidence. He knew the answer to every question Miss Insko asked, and he wasn't shy about raising his hand, shaking it furiously at times until the teacher called on him. Many of the other students resented him, but what could he do about that? He was clearly intellectually superior to everybody here—why hide it?

He would have received even more stars, perhaps, if his answers had not been so lengthy, and if he had been able to avoid digressions when answering.

After discussing Mark Twain, Miss Insko devoted the rest of the class to a general discussion of other famous American writers. When Ernest Hemingway came up, Leon shared the following anecdote with his class:

DURING THE FIRST WORLD WAR, WHEN HE WAS DRIVING AN AMBULANCE IN ITALY, HEMINGWAY HAD A HABIT OF PLAYING THE AMBULANCE RADIO SO LOUD NONE OF THE WOUNDED WOULD RIDE WITH HIM.

FED UP WITH COMPLAINTS HE WAS RECEIVING FROM INJURED SOLDIERS RETURNING FROM THE FRONT, HEMINGWAY'S COMMANDING OFFICER CALLED HIM INTO

COMPANY HEADQUARTERS ONE AFTERNOON AND DEMANDED HE LOWER THE VOLUME.

"I BEG YOUR PARDON?" HEMINGWAY SAID.

"TURN IT DOWN."

"EXCUSE ME?"

"THE RADIO."

"HUH?"

"IT'S TOO DAMN LOUD!"

"I CAN'T UNDERSTAND YOU," HEMINGWAY SAID. "I HAVE GUMDROPS IN MY EARS."

"YOU HAVE WHAT IN YOUR EARS?"

"GUMDROPS, SIR."

"WHAT IN GOD'S NAME ARE YOU DOING WITH GUM-DROPS IN YOUR EARS?"

"THEY BLOCK OUT THE NOISE FROM MY AMBULANCE RADIO. IT'S DEAFENING."

Miss Insko thought the story "charming," though she chastised Leon for his use of the *d*-word. "Where exactly did you hear that story?" she asked him.

"Hear it?" Leon said. "I don't remember hearing it anywhere."

"Where did you read it, then?"

"I don't remember reading it anywhere."

"Then where did the story come from?"

Leon shrugged. "I haven't the slightest idea."

Perhaps because she was used to dealing with sixth graders, Miss Insko seemed to accept this answer.

Other famous American writers were mentioned that day. When Miss Insko mentioned *Moby Dick*, much of the class giggled.

"Dick?" one of the boys asked loudly. "Did you say 'dick'?" The class broke into a loud round of laughter.

Leon was confused. He didn't understand what was funny.[1] He noticed, however, that Miss Insko appeared slightly embarrassed: her face turned red, and she soon changed the subject.

"Has anyone heard of William Faulkner?" Miss Insko asked. "How about you, Leon?"

"Yes," he said, "I've heard of him."

"Well, sure," someone in the back row said. "He's heard of *all* the writers. But, like, how about letting someone else answer a question, huh?"

The class was silent. "Don't everybody jump in at once," Leon said.

No one spoke, so Leon told them what he knew about William Faulkner. "In a vault next to my bathroom," he said, "I keep an encyclopedia of information so utterly amazing I pull it out only on special occasions, such as when I'm entertaining royalty, building a new bobsled run, or talking to my mother. Anyhow, in the bottom right-hand corner of page 1346 of Volume Seven, 'Einstein's Monkeys–Forensic Lettuce,' is an entry on William Faulkner

---

1. *Years later he still wouldn't. In fact, Tolbert was known throughout the entire NACC system as quite possibly its most naive and gullible instructor. Practical jokes were common in his classes. Students sometimes taped the light switches in the off position and told Tolbert that the maintenance man had just been by and said there was a problem with the electricity. Tolbert believed them and taught his class in the dark. Students often choreographed row-by-row farting sessions, in which one class member after another became flatulent: it was well known to all that Tolbert ignored such excesses, due to his upbringing. One student missed several classes, and each time Tolbert asked him why, he told him, "My aunt died." This happened at least a dozen times over a period of two months. "I'm so sorry," Tolbert habitually said.*

wherein it is noted that the Nobel Prize–winning novelist once made a professional go at—of all things—*acting*. And though it is difficult if not altogether impossible for me to imagine William Faulkner sharing the big screen with Jimmy Stewart, it is nonetheless a documented fact. He did! Furthermore, he was widely praised for it, garnering tremendous acclaim for his touching portrayal of Harvey in the film of the same title. At least that's what it says in my encyclopedia. Between 'Far-Sighted Vampires' and 'Fauna Radar.'"

When Leon finished, he looked at Miss Insko, and she looked back at him, and they quickly found themselves looking at each other: eye contact. Across the distance of the room, Dorothea and Leon stared into each other's eyes and saw in that brief glimpse shared in the space of air between a group of rank sixth graders the vision of a future together, a future consisting of a husband and a wife, of children perhaps, but certainly of love, that or at least a decent facsimile, something approaching love, at any rate, a certain warmth, a kind word on occasion, maybe something more, and maybe something much, much less: very little can be gleaned from a brief glimpse across the room. Still, neither would be the same after that glimpse. The air itself was charged with the transmutation; even the youngsters felt it. In the continuing somewhat awkward silence, one boy raised a shaking hand. Miss Insko nodded in his direction.

"Yes?" she said.

"May I be excused, Miss Insko? I need to use the bath-room."

"Of course," Miss Insko said, returning her gaze to her future husband.

Of course, Leon thought, feeling the urge himself.

CHAPTER 19

Artists,

Authors, and

Advertising

ERNEST HEMINGWAY hawking rifles. Salvador Dali selling wristwatches. Jack Kerouac pitching tires. The world is full of talented individuals who leave the sweatshop of the soul to lend their name and image to a product they believe in—for a price. And yet each time it happens, the pure in spirit—those people, that is, who only do things they really and truly believe in, *really and truly*—have something to say about it. "Sellout!" they scream. "Has-been!" And, of course, that most dreaded cry of the pure in spirit: "May I borrow some money? Please?"

But it should come as no surprise to those who are not easily surprised that this has been so throughout history. Many people—writers, artists, composers, musicians—have traded in on the celebrity their talent earned them.

Henry David Thoreau did it. After *Walden* made him very nearly a household word in this country, Thoreau was paid $250—no small amount of change back then—to appear in a magazine advertisement. Beneath a photograph of him sleeping by Walden Pond he is quoted as saying: "After a long walk in the woods, my feet often throb with a truly unnatural pain. That's when I apply a healthy covering of Dickerson's Soothing Salve. It works! I'm back walking again—and writing—in no time!"

And Pablo Picasso's role in making Zesty Cola the most popular brand of soft drink in pre–World War II America is a textbook case of name-image association. On billboards everywhere Picasso's cubist self-portrait could be seen proclaiming, "During my blue periods, I often reach into the icebox for a refreshing Zesty Cola. What a pick-me-up! It gives me a completely new outlook on life!"

In 1722, Daniel Defoe was one of London's most celebrated writers. *Robinson Crusoe* was hugely popular, and so was its author. And yet Defoe did not realize much of a profit, even with hardcover sales in the thousands—a goodly number in the eighteenth century. The only real money he made, in fact, was when he allowed a company selling cough syrup to attach his likeness to an advertisement they ran in *The Observer* and, beneath it, these words: "Next time I'm stranded on a desert island, I'll be sure to take a bottle of Superior Anti-Coughing Solution with me. It really works!"

And even these are relatively recent examples. Among his many farsighted inspirations, Leonardo da Vinci invented the leaflet and could be seen on many a Florentine corner handing them out to passersby. Even earlier, Plato had Aristotle advertise his school of philosophy by going to the center of an Athens agora and peripatetically shouting about it. "So you want to be a philosopher," he'd cry out, "but you don't have the time? Well, maybe you don't know what time really *is*. We can teach you. Come on down to Plato's and see us soon! It really works!"

And it really did.

A TRUE STORY. *Some years after he became well known for his films—and for his corpulent figure—Alfred Hitchcock went on a diet and lost one hundred seventeen pounds. The egg-shaped body the world had come to associate with him disappeared completely, and in its place was a svelte, dashing Gregory Peck-ish sort of Alfred Hitchcock.*

He looked great.

Unfortunately, he became unrecognizable. The men who stood guard at the gates of the movie studios refused to let him in on occasion, and when he did get in, actors and actresses alike laughed at him when he tried to tell them what to do.

C H A P T E R

"Why should I do that, string bean?" one famous actress is quoted as saying.

Hitchcock tried to gain back the weight he had lost, but the diet had been too great a success: he could only gain a pound or two a week, and at that rate, he knew, he would lose everything. Indeed, he was very nearly ruined. Then he remembered a trick he had used in one of his early movies; he had made a young thin man age into an old fat one. And from that day on, he stuffed pillows inside his shirt to make himself look like the fatso we know him to have been today.

This is a little known story. But it's true. Hitchcock stuffed pillows into his shirt. Hitchcock was actually a very thin man. Tell all your friends.

—L.T., DATE UNKNOWN

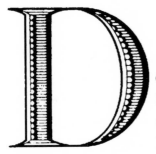OROTHEA LEE INSKO was born in Mayo, Ohio, the fourth of five daughters, to Efrom and Anne Insko. The Inskos were straw farmers; they sold their crop to gardeners, basket weavers, furniture manufacturers, and others who, for one reason or another, needed straw. From the moment he married Anne, Efrom made no secret of the fact that he wanted her to bear a boy—lots of them, if she could—because a boy would be a great help on the straw farm. A boy could gather the straw, bind it, weigh it, then truck it to market; a girl, he felt, just didn't have the same ability. And so they tried and tried again. As each month passed and his wife got bigger, Efrom would pass the time in the straw field imagining what his son would look like and what a help he would be with the straw, until his wife would call to him—"Efrom! I think he's acoming!"—and he would once again face his disappointment, which came to him in the form of another girl. When his wife exhorted him to take the girls out into the field, he balked.

"Strawin' ain't for ladies," he said. "I never want to see one of my little girls out there. And I mean never."

And he never did. He ended up doing all of the strawing himself until the day he died, under the hot August sun, gathering straw.

Following the death of her husband, Anne sold the farm to a huge straw conglomerate and took her family into town.

She was able to send Dorothea to the university—the first daughter who had expressed any interest at all in going— after which Dorothea came back to Mayo and became a teacher. Unfortunately, soon after she returned, the entire town was lost to a great fire—known today as the Great Fire in Mayo—and through the good services of a fireman she met, she was able to land a job in Pelham, New York, where only one year later she met Leon Tolbert, whom she married in a small, traditional ceremony at Saint Luke's Episcopal Church.

But while the marriage ceremony was traditional, the courtship was not. Perhaps only Leon Tolbert could have wooed a woman in the way he did and won her; no doubt if anyone else had attempted it he would have looked foolish and ridiculous. But looking foolish and ridiculous seemed to become Leon Tolbert, then as later in life.

Where some other man might have penned letters of love, Tolbert wrote small essays on some of his favorite authors and sent them to Dorothea tucked between the pages of overdue library books, which she had to return, reluctantly paying the fine. But to Tolbert this was merely incidental. It was his words that mattered.

"You couldn't always write about sex," he once wrote her. "For a long time you had to rely on metaphor to get your point across. For example, I remember reading *Madame Bovary* in school and, clever young scholar that I was, wondering out loud in class one morning, and for the benefit of all the other clever young scholars assembled there with me, why so many lustful couples in nineteenth-century novels seemed to spend so much of their time riding around the countryside in closed carriages, which always seemed to be rocking mercilessly back and forth despite the lack of any potholes dotting the landscape. My instructor, Mrs. Turcot, who generally did not find my inquiries to be nearly as clever as I did, for once actually appeared to take some interest in what I was asking. She paused to speculate: 'The carriages rocked back and forth,' she said, 'because their occupants were rocking back and forth. And their occupants were rocking back and forth because the carriages had wheels that were made of wood, not rubber.' And with a look that gave no hint of any deeper understanding, Mrs. Turcot asked us all to open our books to page three-thirteen, whereupon a discussion of Emma Bovary's eating habits summarily ensued."

What exactly *was* this? Dorothea wondered when she received Leon's missive. A romantic essay? A literary letter? A weird confession? No matter. It had been signed and sent by Leon, and that was good enough for her. As each day brought a new note—and a new overdue library book—she became

more and more intrigued by Leon's unique approach to courtship.

"Do you think it would be possible to have a regular conversation with Dorothy Parker?" he once wrote her. "A conversation in which, after you said something like, 'Peter and I are considering a separation,' she was able to reply, 'Oh, my dear,' instead of, 'A separation? How silly of me. I didn't even know you were married!' But it wasn't in her to play the straight guy, was it? Though Lord knows she wished it were, if only for a few minutes each day. She used to wake up in the middle of the night, grab a notebook by her bed and scribble down conversations she'd had in a dream—dry, lifeless conversations with people who should have known better:

Benchley: Hello, Dorothy!

Parker: Hello!

Benchley: How was your day?

Parker: Fine. Yours?

Benchley: Swell.

"This passage, by the way, from Dorothy Parker's secret notebook, *Just Call Me Dot, Darn It,* was typical of her fantasies. Later in that same volume, she laments, 'Like a caged animal, I am frequently approached by friends and strangers who, winking and grinning at each other as they await my droll reply, say, "So tell us, Miss Parker, how are you today?"'"

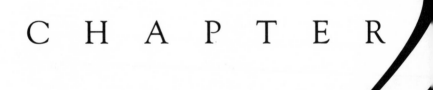

CHAPTER 2

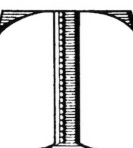OLBERT'S UNRAVELING sent a shudder through the NACC campus. No one could remember the last time the college had undergone such an odd, nasty trauma, unless it was when the entire sewage system got backed up the year before, or when a flock of swallows nested in Mrs. Dannemeyer's classroom, or when Sparky the Frisbee Dog caught his last flying disk, zigging through the rush-hour traffic, dying from a final failure to zag. Tolbert's last days were just as sordid and emotionally stirring. Had some other professor been facing his mental breakdown, it would have been said of him, "He's not himself anymore." With Tolbert, however, this was not quite the case. As odd and disturbing a person as he'd become, he was still himself, only more so: he was Tolbert times ten, ultra-Tolbert, ur-Tolbert.

He no longer addressed his class from a lectern in the front of the room; he now began his talks from the last seat in the last row, sometimes singing loudly, sometimes nearly whispering. His students had resigned themselves long ago to the fact that the subject they were there to learn—remedial English—would probably never be mentioned. Now they had to resign themselves to not even hearing what the professor was saying. It was a difficult period for many of his students, as they watched him disintegrate: one girl was sent home, having a bad case of the nerves; another asked if she could go back to high school. Andy Panetta remembers the day they played musical chairs—with no music. It was an easy time for nobody, and handouts like this one were becoming the norm rather than the exception:

LITERARY MILESTONES: A CHRONOLOGY

41018 B.C. Paleolithic scholars produce what is thought to be the first dictionary. Unfortunately, no words have been coined to go into it.

31344 B.C. On a cave wall in what is now northern Europe, a Cro-Magnon hunter scratches these words: "For a good time, call Grok." Personals, as we know them, are born.

3034 B.C. Lugalzaggisi, writing about his bloody conquest of Sumeria, rhymes the words "flay" and "slay" in successive sentences. He then rhymes "bed" with "dead," "fry" with "cry," "frail" with "impale," and "burn" with "urn." The result is one of the world's oldest known poems. It's also one of the world's worst.

1761 B.C. King Hammurabi devises his famous code. From that day forward no one is able to understand him.

A.D. 1 Roman theater begins at Leptis Magna in North Africa. The premier production closes after just three nights, however, the victim of bad reviews and competition from a nearby coliseum franchise, where season tickets to all gladiator fights are being offered at half price.

A.D. 185 Pausanias, one of the earliest known geographers, completes his ten-volume *Description of Greece*. The work is widely praised and, predictably, offered as a membership premium for the Tablet-of-the-Month Club.

A.D. 1545   Roger Ascham publishes *Toxophilus*. After soar-
ing to the number one spot on *The Spectator*'s
best-seller list, the book quickly plummets
into obscurity once the public realizes it is about
archery and not the plague.

Meanwhile, Tolbert's colleagues were meeting with administration officials as they tried to come to terms with the situation. The most often asked question at the proceedings was
"Who hired this guy in the first place?" No one seemed to
know. And then it dawned on them that Tolbert hadn't been
hired at all—he'd simply shown up one day and started
teaching.

"That's impossible," someone said. "You just can't show up
somewhere and start teaching. Not even at NACC."

"Yeah. They made me show my driver's license and everything," a professor of philosophy said.

But this indeed is what had happened: Tolbert had merely
dropped in, found an empty classroom, and started talking.

"If he was never hired—" someone began.

"Then he—he . . . can't be fired!"

"*Oh, my God.*" Someone ran screaming from the room.

And it was in this light that Leon Tolbert began to seem
like a fact of life, a human persistence who would exist as
long as they themselves existed. Only half jokingly then did
a department chairman suggest destroying the entire campus.
A few people laughed. A few others wondered what, exactly,
would be involved in such a procedure. It is a tribute to the
entire Northern Arizona Community College system that
cooler heads prevailed. The campus remains intact to this day.

While Franz Kafka was arguably one of the best writers the twentieth century has produced, what is not arguable is that he had the best name. Franz Kafka. What we wouldn't give for a name like that! Just to be able to sign our letters, "Sincerely, Franz Kafka." Or better yet, "K."

"See you later, K."

C H A P T E R 2

About his work. In many ways, Franz Kafka's stories and novels are incredibly depressing; they leave us feeling uneasy. But sometimes he would have small parties where he would read from his work. And he brought the house down! His guests laughed—until they cried! This is true! Kafka was hilarious! Today we think how bleak, how black, but back then, in his living room, it was "Oh, Kafka, please! You're killing me! I can't stop laughing!"

Franz . . . Kafka.

—L.T., MARCH 26, 1993

PRING CAME, and with it young Leon Tolbert's pen seemed to blossom like a flower. Dorothea was soon receiving two or three of his "lovely sketches," as she liked to call them, each day.

"Wasn't it my mother who told me that life was a series of compromises," began one such sketch, "that what I do and what I love to do may be two entirely different things, and that after three days both fish and company begin to smell?

"Indeed.

"And now, as I grow older, I find that—heaven forbid—Mom may have been right. For wasn't it I who for years held up Sir Arthur Conan Doyle as my supreme exemplar? Here's a gentleman who spent his life writing the most wonderful detective stories. Sherlock Holmes and Dr. Watson! What a pair! To have stumbled upon these characters before anybody else, and to have written about them day after day, morning, noon, and night! You know, I said, maybe I can do that too!

"But what's this?

"I can't!

"And why not? Because I'm hungry and need to eat, and the grocery store cashier prefers money to mysteries!"

Certainly Tolbert the writer did not send these pastiches without thought; nor is it fair to surmise, as some have, that he was simply using Dorothea as a captive reader. No, Tolbert knew what he was doing. He was wooing a woman who, he believed, shared his love of literature.

What better way to worm his way into her heart?

Unfortunately, Tolbert was, as it turned out, dead wrong; even though Dorothea was a teacher of English, she had no particular fondness for that language or any other. Becoming a teacher had for her been a matter of convenience, and by no means a calling. Her interest in attending college had been limited to an intense desire to get off the straw farm and meet young men; going back to Mayo had been her worst nightmare, and yet at the time she seemed to have no other choice. Some say, in fact, that it was she who started the fire which consumed the town, though there was never any proof of that.[1] Her state of mind—vague boredom—as she read Leon's pieces was not what Tolbert had imagined it would be, and yet it seemed to achieve the final sought-after effect.

Tolbert continued attending Dorothea's class and even began helping her with some of her duties; within a month after meeting her, young Leon was grading Dorothea's students' homework assignments and making up quizzes.

Toward the end of the school year, Leon, on one occasion, substitute-taught for Miss Inkso, to the consternation of the school's principal and every parent of every student in the class, who complained that the children had all come home speaking of themselves in the second person plural. Miss Inkso almost lost her job as a result, but by that time she didn't

---

1. There was some speculation in Mayo that a fireman may have discovered evidence that Dorothea Insko set the fire on purpose: a smoldering brassiere found at the fire's source. The evidence was later lost, however, and it is believed Dorothea may have had some sort of romantic attachment to this fireman, who, as noted elsewhere in this volume, eventually helped her find a job in Pelham, New York. Records indicate that the fireman was himself working on relocating to the Pelham area when he fell in love with another of the Insko sisters, Patsy. They were the only couple to remain in Mayo after it burned down. He became mayor, and she became police chief. During difficult marital periods he would demote her, and she would have him arrested. They had several children. Since none of them left Mayo and no one else moved there, they intermarried and had lots of strange children. Mayo existed until the early 1980s when it once again burned down, this time taking the entire Insko clan with it.

care: she was engaged to Leon Tolbert, her star student, and she would soon be living a life of great luxury, for she was about to marry the heir of one of the wealthiest men in town.

This, at any rate, is what Leon told her, or somehow implied to her through his conversation, though after they were married he denied it. He suggested that she had simply misinterpreted one of his "lovely sketches" and left it at that. Dorothea was never able to forget it, however, and for this reason she often mockingly called him Sir Leon up to and until the day he died.[2]

The fact that Leon Tolbert was able to find a wife at all filled him with hope and gave him the courage he needed to follow his dream. The wedding was beautiful, and Leon didn't forget the ring, but through it all he could not help thinking that everything that had gone before was over and that on this day he was starting anew. From this moment forward, his life would be brighter, happier, and more successful. It is only with the hindsight time has afforded us that we can look back at the somewhat naive Leon and think, Sorry.

---

2. *The question remains as to why Dorothea didn't seek a divorce from Leon after she discovered not only that he was not of royal lineage but that both he and his parents were still in debt to the encyclopedia company Leon had once worked for.*

CHAPTER 2

3

AFTER COMPLETING THE SCARLET LETTER, HAWTHORNE
WENT ON STRIKE.

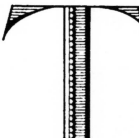HE FACULTY MEETING ended when it was decided that a recon-naissance team consisting of three professors and one administrator visit Tolbert's classroom for an offi-cial observation.

On this day Tolbert had resumed his formal position behind the lectern. His hair was combed back out of his eyes, and his tie was knotted. When the four observers entered the classroom, Tolbert squinted to see who they were, and, recognizing them, he waved. The students sat in their chairs taking notes. All seemed well—until the observers sat down and listened.

"And so," Tolbert continued, "Pablo Picasso's desire to succeed in the world of big business was never to be fulfilled, but it wasn't for lack of trying. Like many men who have conquered their particular field of endeavor, Picasso felt hemmed in by his status as an artist: he wanted more. He wanted to be a businessman.

"His first great failure was a line of sport coats. His second was a line of shoes, the designs of which were inspired by some of his cubist works. Not easily dissuaded, he continued plugging away in the fashion world, following the shoes and sport coats with an entire collection of men's suits called That Picasso Kind of Look, which was a complete failure all over the world.

"Eventually he left fashion behind and concentrated on investments. Picasso had an uncanny knack for investing in companies just as they were about to go bankrupt, and he did this on any number of occasions, losing untold millions of francs. His only business success, a relatively minor one, came when he opened a small shop in Nice, called Pablo's Hair Weaves. He had hopes of franchising one day, but, alas, this was never to be."

Tolbert removed his glasses and cleaned them with a tissue.

"Isn't he the remedial English instructor?" one professor whispered to the other.

"I thought so," he said. "But did you know that about Picasso? I had no idea."

"Sure, I knew," the administrator said.

"Now, where were we?" Tolbert said.

A student raised his hand. "You were going to tell us about the Melville-Hawthorne correspondence," he said.

"So I was! Thank you.[1] The creative process is a long and arduous one, and excerpts from letters Melville wrote to Hawthorne provide sufficient illustration that this is so."

"'Dear Hawthorne,' one letter begins. 'I've conceived of a grand idea for a truly grand novel. It's rather vague now, but I think it will concern the adventures of some sort of fisherman. One day his nose is bitten off by an insane dolphin, and the rest of the book will be about his quest to find the dolphin and retrieve his nose.'

EXCERPTS FROM MELVILLE'S LETTERS PROVIDE SUFFICIENT ILLUSTRATION THAT THE CREATIVE PROCESS IS A LONG AND ARDUOUS ONE.

"'Dear Nathaniel,' he writes in a letter two months later, 'Thank you for your criticism. You're absolutely right: the dolphin is wrong, and the body part is wrong. I've changed the entire book now so that it's a rather large flounder which

1. *By this time Tolbert's state of mind had been assimilated by his students. He no longer seemed different and strange to them, for they too had become different and strange. They were able to understand him and his thought processes, often knowing what he was going to say before he did himself. Some would say this was proof that his father's theory of osmotics truly worked. Others would say the students were simply caving in to the intense psychotic pressure.*

nips off the fisherman's thumb. Oh: and the flounder (in order to distinguish it from other flounders) is colored a funny sort of mauve. What do you think?'

"'Dear Nate,' Melville writes after hearing from Hawthorne, 'You're right, you're right! It's not going to work with the flounder. It's got to be something big, *really* big. But what? Send me some sort of a suggestion soon: if we stumble upon the right sort of sea creature, this could be an enormous book.'"

The four observers in the back of the classroom caucused again.

"I *know* he made that up," one said. "I've read everything Melville wrote. He never—"

"Are you sure?" the administrator said. "It sounds darned authentic to me."

"Well, the creative process *is* long and arduous," the other professor said. "That's why I avoid it. I think he hit the nail on the head there."

"I seem to have lost my place," Tolbert said, smiling at his class, looking, indeed, very much lost.

"So have we," they said, smiling back.

"Then I suppose . . . class is over."

"Then we suppose it's over, too," they said.

And they rose and left, and Tolbert stood there watching. Something seemed to come to him then, and he raised his hand as if to stop them. Then he shook his head—it was nothing, nothing—gathered his notes, and walked away.

Sidonie Gabrielle Colette, onetime president of L'Académie Goncourt and the recipient of Marcel Proust's critical praise, began her distinguished career as a ghostwriter for her husband. We mention this not to belittle Colette's stature as a novelist but rather to amplify our own. You see we too began our career as a ghostwriter, not for our spouse but for our employer, the president of an esteemed institution of higher learning, who at this very moment is probably passed out on a houseboat parked just off the coast of Tahiti. Unlike Colette, however, who went on to publish such exquisite novels as La Chatte, *we ourselves appear to have hit a dead end in the world of letters. Locked behind a steel door in our Flagstaff research facility, we*

C H A P T E R 2

sit pecking away at an old Underwood typewriter, contriving page after page of phony biographies and waiting for that big call from Redbook. Are we bitter? We are not. Bitterness becomes no one, not even our employer. Thank God he's too stupid to read our— Hey, what's going on? Like, close the door. You're letting in light! Whoaa! Whooaaaa! Let go! We were just kid—

—L.T., FEBRUARY 24, 1993

COLETTE BEGAN AS A GHOSTWRITER.

OW THAT Leon Tolbert was married, it was time for his career to take off like a rocket. It was time for him to be hired by some prestigious Ivy League university to lecture on the great thinkers of all time. It was time for him to become recognized for his unique style of teaching and, with some alacrity, to work his way up through the teaching ranks, receive tenure, the chairmanship of his department, and finally, the Pulitzer Prize for his *Collected Essays*. As he lay dying in his bed, surrounded by well-wishers, including the president of the United States, he would take his wife's hand in his and say, "Ah, Death is a rumpled, humpbacked thing with no sense of humor." Whereupon he would close his eyes and pass from this world to the next, content that he had done all there was do here on earth, that he'd had a dream and that he'd lived that dream, and that now it was time to move on.

But before all this could happen, he needed to come out of the bathroom. His wife was begging him.

"Is everything okay, Leon?"

"Everything is fine."

"You've been in there for two hours. Don't you think—"

"Has it been two hours?"

"Over two hours."

"It hasn't seemed like two hours. Really. It's seemed more like forty-five minutes. Maybe fifty."

"That's not the point," Dorothea said.

"I realize that, dear."

"The point—"

"I think I know the point," Leon said. "I'm the one who's sitting here, after all. Of all people, I think the point would be clearest to me."

"Why not come out, then?"

"Because I'm not done," he responded.

"Leon," she said somewhat impatiently, "if nothing has happened in two hours, nothing is going to happen at all."

"That's your opinion," he said.

And on and on it went, in a vein very similar to this, for some time, until Dorothea got tired and walked away. The truth is, he had long ago given up doing anything constructive in an excretory sense. For the last hour and a half he had been writing. Writing samples might be nice to have if he could put them together and send them to an Ivy League school where it snowed all the time and where they could see in his work that thing which he was sure was there, that special thing, which only someone really exceptionally well trained could be expected to see, that divine spark of—dare he use the word?—afflatus. He dared to use it. Afflatus. Leon Tolbert had afflatus! It was true. He wished he could let the world know this: he wished he could write it on billboards, on buildings, on bathroom walls! He wished others saw what he saw when he saw his own work.

Afflatus.

CHAPTER

"Mrs. Tolbert?"

"Yes?"

"This is Harland Lowell, from NACC."

"Yes?"

"Your husband, Leon, works here."

"Yes?"

"For some time now, Mrs. Tolbert, Leon hasn't been acting in a manner that his colleagues and school officials feel is appropriate for an instructor."

"Did he deliver that lecture on his head?"

"I beg your pardon?"

"This morning he said he was going to deliver a lecture standing on his head. I said, 'Leon, don't. Please don't. You'll fall on somebody. You'll hurt your neck. Who needs a man standing on his head?' But he did it anyway, didn't he?"

"To my knowledge, no."

"Then he listens to me. Thank God for that."

"Mrs. Tolbert, with each passing day, the situation is becoming more and more serious."

"I'm surprised you've put up with it this long."

"Well, it's not so much a question of putting up with it, Mrs. Tolbert."

"It has been for me."

"I understand."

"Do you really?"

"To the degree that I'm another human being and share the same emotions you do, I think—"

"You don't share the same bathroom. Until you share the

same bathroom with Leon Tolbert, there is no way you can understand."

"That may be."

"He's always loved the bathroom, Mr. Hole."

"Lowell."

"He used to work in the bathroom. Now he posts little notes in there."

"Mrs. Tolbert, I—"

"Listen," she said. "He taped this to the toilet seat yesterday: 'Delmore Schwartz was only twenty-five when his first book was published. The title of the book was *In Dreams Begin Responsibilities*, an idea that, for better or worse, was taken literally by many East Coast cognoscenti. "What did I do with that fish?" they might be heard muttering to their wives. "Fish?" "Yeah, the one that was in my hat in the big room with the blue curtains." Soon readers everywhere were

trying to take responsibility for their dreams, and scores of people went crazy trying. Schwartz finally had to make a public announcement that it was just a story, for God's sake, not a fact of life, and that he had no intention of running for public office.'"

"That was taped to the toilet?"

"And listen to this one. I found it crumpled up inside the medicine cabinet: 'So we're in the checkout lane at the supermarket one day and read this headline: "Amelia Earhart Found Alive on Desert Island—Sex Slave to Ape Man for Half a Century!" Our first instinct is to laugh; we've seen these things before. But then suddenly we realize that's no tabloid; that's the cover of *Time* magazine we're looking at! *It must be true*. The force of the news is too strong and baffling. We drop the magazine and the can of cat food we were holding, and the man in front of us picks it up. "There you go," he says with a smile. Oh, my God, it's Elvis! He hands us the cat food, but before we can say anything he's gone, swept through the checkout lane in an instant by a fastidious cashier who turns out to be *Adolf Hitler!*

'"Paper or plastic?" he asks us menacingly.

'We can't decide. The line behind us is getting longer. Marilyn Monroe is there, shopping with JFK. They're all starting to complain.

'"Paper or plastic?" he asks us again. "Which will it be?"

'"Amelia Earhart," we say, showing him the magazine. "She's alive."

'"Yes," he says, laughing and gesturing for Liberace to put his groceries on the counter. "Paper or plastic?"'

"Mr. Hole?"

"Mrs. Toll Booth?"

"Tolbert."

"Lowell."

"I'm worried, too."

"And with good reason. Leon is crying for help."

"Yes, I suppose he is. At least figuratively."

"And literally too, I'm afraid. That's why I phoned. We need you to come down to the campus."

"What's the matter?"

"Your husband is in a tree."

The early recordings of Glenn Gould continue to inundate the marketplace, many of them having been released against the wishes of the Gould estate, which has set strict guidelines concerning the posthumous release of any and all material. After Gould's death in 1982, many fine recordings were released, including The Glenn Gould Legacy in 1985. At the same time, a cache was discovered of some of his less classical but certainly more popular efforts, including the sound track to the failed Halloween special Ghoulish Gould. Among the songs included here—

CHAPTER 2

none of which met the guidelines established by the Gould estate—are "When Mr. Pumpkin Comes to Town," "Witches Are Scary People," and "I'm Sorry, Mrs. Cavendish, I Thought That Was a Mask." Equally disturbing to the estate were Gould's renditions of some rock 'n' roll favorites, including Glenn Does Elvis and Cool Gould, an eclectic compilation of some of Isaac Hayes's greatest hits. Gould made these recordings during—how shall we say?—hard times and thought the tapes of these sessions had been destroyed. Unfortunately, this was not the case.

—L.T., APRIL 14, 1993

6

GLENN DOES ELVIS.

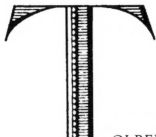OLBERT SOON found he produced his best writing while sitting on the toilet, and for the next several months he would wake, drink a single cup of coffee, eat a lightly buttered slice of toast, and retire to the water closet for the remainder of the day. If, by some unlucky chance, Dorothea happened to be in there at the same time, he expected her prompt withdrawal, regardless of whether she was "finished" or not. This is what she would often say when he knocked at the locked door: "But, Leon, I'm not *finished!*" To which he would respond, "And I have not begun."[1] Similarly, if she needed to use the facilities while he was "working," she was out of luck. She was occasionally seen dashing to one or another neighbor's house an hour or so after lunch. Friends of Mrs. Tolbert characterize those first few months of marriage as "extremely unpleasant" for her "in almost every conceivable way."

Meanwhile, Leon Tolbert struggled with his work. He often wrote three thousand words a day, much of which he flushed down the commode. Still, some of the surviving material

---

1. *It was unclear exactly what he meant by this. Dorothea asked him, "And what is that supposed to mean?" But he would never say. He was, at times, purposefully recondite to no real end. His friends said he liked the idea of being misunderstood, and thus he strove to create that image, the model of a misunderstood man. "What Leon never really grasped," a colleague of his who wishes to remain anonymous has said, "is that the main thing about misunderstood individuals is that they speak a kind of sense. Leon was misunderstood simply because he said silly things. There is a difference."*

shows merit. And while it is tempting, certainly, to refer to what remains as juvenilia, one must remember that Tolbert was already in his early twenties by then; it was a point in his career that scholars interested in Tolbert and the Tolbertian drama generally refer to as the Bathroom Period.

Although the uniqueness and scholarly panache Tolbert brought to his subjects was possibly without parallel in academe and in journals associated with it, the question remains: to what end was he writing? As the days stretched into weeks and the weeks stretched into months and the bathroom still had a permanent Occupied sign scrawled across the door, there was no immediate indication—to Leon, his wife, or anybody else—that his efforts were adding up to anything at all.

"Perhaps it's appropriate that I write in the john," Leon wrote in the john one day. "For what I am writing seems to be little more than a big pile of horseshit."

Tolbert's feelings about his work weren't helping his marriage, either. Dorothea had a short affair with their next-door neighbor, Martin Stroup, but she later said it was merely an affair of convenience, as Mr. Stroup's bathroom was closer than any other. Leon, of course, never found out about this. He was too immersed in his own life to think about his wife's. Some other man would have let himself go at this point. Some other man would have stopped shaving, showering, brushing his hair. But since Leon was in the bathroom all day, this was impossible. He usually shaved twice before noon and took showers more often than that. If nothing else, he was well groomed and spotless.

And perhaps he *was* nothing else. In the glow of the bathroom light, as he stared at himself in the mirror, it was this thought that plagued him most: Leon Tolbert—all style, no substance. He was running head-on into an intellectual crisis of the most severe proportions. Sure, he could write a few clever lines about someone, but could he write an entire chapter? He doubted it. His train of thought, it seemed, was limited to a paragraph or at most a page; he was apparently incapable of the sustained concentration required to produce an in-depth analysis of a subject as taxing as, say, Dreiser or Mann or Dante or Nabokov. He studied what he had written, and the feeling it left him with was that he was wasting his time, that he had no more business writing essays than his wife had— Hey, where *was* his wife?

"Dorothea!"

"Yes."

"Would you bring me a bowl of soup?"

"I'm waxing the floor. You'll have to wait a few minutes."

He waited, but soon forgot what he was waiting for. An egg cream? His bathrobe? The morning paper? Some shoe polish? Did it even matter? Indeed, these were harsh, unforgiving times for Leon Tolbert, and it was in this depressed state of mind that he wrote the following:

The daughter of Irish immigrants, Sarah Longley Farraday was born illiterate and nearly mute. Gradually, however, she learned to speak and read, and by the time she was five years old, she'd acquired a working vocabulary.

Her early life—like most of her middle, late, and afterlife—is shrouded in mystery and lack of interest. But the records clearly show that Sarah had many fascinating ideas for poems, short stories, and novels. Ideas which, in the presence of her family, she would often mention in passing, as if they were nothing.

And in a way, they were.

"I have this idea for a plot," she once told her brother Jerome. "A young man gets into a bit of trouble with the authorities. But he's entirely innocent of any wrongdoing. He then falls in love with his attorney, a beautiful young woman, who as it turns out is also the mayor's niece. And the police chief's mistress. Well, one thing leads to another, and—what do you know?—happy ending!"

Sarah was sixteen years old when she had this idea. Critics are unsure what form it would have taken had she ever opted to write it, but a good guess is that it would have best lent itself to being either a novel or a play; Sarah would have been intimate with both.

In her late teens, Sarah had other ideas. One, which she shared with a college English instructor, went something like this: "A woman is born to poor immigrant parents who work hard to put her through school and who constantly make sure that nothing bad happens to her. And nothing does. Until one afternoon . . ."

This is where the idea ended, though it's safe to say that, with sufficient time and effort, it could have been developed into something much larger, more complex. Had she only written it!

In her early twenties, Sarah met Edwin Farraday, an accountant for some of the largest theaters on Broadway, and she married him in a private ceremony near Greenwich, Connecticut, where he had a large home on a sprawling country estate. Over the next several years, Edwin nurtured Sarah's artistic inclinations, to the extent that he actually wrote her ideas down in a notebook that he kept beside his bed.

"September 21, 1941. Today Sarah had a remarkable idea for a book. It had to do with a young man being sent off to war. The implications were astonishing!"

Or this entry: "August 30, 1937. Sarah told me about an idea she had for a musical. It was truly wonderful. I can actually see it being performed in my mind's eye, or rather on my mind's stage, at this very instant. Would that it might be written!"

Would that it might be: Would that those were the words written on Sarah Longley Farraday's tombstone. For she never wrote a word in her life.

Something about this particular piece sickened Tolbert; it was fortunate he was in the bathroom at the time he wrote it. Sarah Farraday had never existed, and for all practical purposes, neither had he. For the past three months he had been stuck in this shiny-tiled room writing his little nothings and the world had kept turning; people had lived and died; the community colleges in every state across the country had somehow plodded along. If he disappeared today, what difference would it make to anybody? His wife might appreciate free access to the bath, but other than that? Next to nothing. In a moment this truth was revealed to him: he wouldn't be teaching at Harvard anytime soon. Not even at Rutgers. What did he expect? A nominating committee to knock down his bathroom door searching for him? What kind of ugly dream world had he been living in?

Well, he told himself, no more! There was only one person who would see to it that Leon Tolbert got what he deserved: that person was Leon Tolbert. He would take fate in his hands. Instead of waiting for something to happen, he would make it happen. And though he might never give his Norton Lectures, he would position himself. He would work himself up.

"Dorothea!" he cried through the door. "I'm coming out!"

"Oh, Leon!" she called back.

And they embraced in the freshly waxed hallway, as if a long journey had only now ended, and another was ripe to begin.

CHAPTER

THOMAS WOLFE: THE MAN, THE MYTH, THE MAILBOX.

AT FIRST, Dorothea Tolbert remembers, she didn't think she had understood Mr. Lowell correctly. *Your husband is on his knees? Your husband has fleas? Your husband is eating peas?* Finally, however, she realized that Leon was in a tree. She felt somewhat better knowing his class was there, at the bottom of the tree, listening as he gave his lecture. At least he's not just sitting in a tree, she thought. At least he's doing something. Keeping busy: this was always a good sign. Mr. Lowell had not really considered it as such, however; he felt her presence was needed immediately, so she'd hopped in the car and driven over to the NACC campus. She was willing to do whatever she could; it was just that Lowell had neglected to tell her *which* tree. And so, while her husband was lecturing from one tree, Mrs. Tolbert was looking up them all, calling, "Leon? Are you up there, Leon?" until finally she saw a group of students huddled about the base of an oak, staring skyward.

It was odd the way this strange state of affairs was made to seem almost normal. The kids were listening intently, taking notes, while this disembodied voice floated down on them.

". . . And so we would say that Thomas Wolfe is one of the last great writers of the modern era who's attained a kind of mythic stature: he's the Paul Bunyan of southern literature. Physically, he was a big man—huge, even; some say monstrous. Could he fit through a door? Possibly, depending on how big the door was. And of course stories abound. His manuscript for *Look Homeward, Angel* is said to have been eighty-five thousand pages long; it was delivered to Maxwell Perkins in shopping carts over a period of a week and stored on the top floor of the Scribner's Building. But Perkins read the whole thing, eventually editing it down to one word: 'Howdy!'"

Can you name three stories by O. Henry other than "The Gift of the Magi"? Not so easy, is it? Know why? Because "The Gift of the Magi" is the only story O. Henry ever wrote. You don't believe us? Well, how about if we told you that O. Henry's real name wasn't William Sydney Porter, as has widely been reported, but rather William Henry Harrison, and that he was not just an author but the ninth president of the United States! Sure, you've probably heard the legend that O. Henry started writing while serving time in Ohio for embezzlement, but the truth is, O. Henry—or rather President O. Henry—never set foot in Ohio, and embezzlement was the furthest thing from his mind when he "borrowed" that money. Fact is, O. Henry took the loot

C H A P T E R

only because he thought it would be very ironic for him not to, though irony, ironically enough, is what he's remembered for most. Anyhow, after he got out of the slammer, President O. Henry moved to Mexico and stole a horse, whom he named Eleanor, and it was Eleanor, not O. Henry, who penned the many wonderful tales we now associate with the brief term of office of the ninth U.S. president.

—L.T., APRIL 1, 1993

CAN YOU NAME THREE STORIES BY O. HENRY OTHER THAN

"THE GIFT OF THE MAGI"?

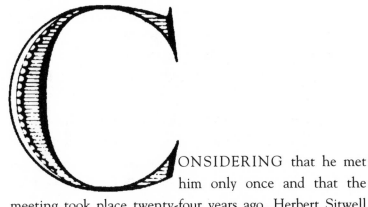ONSIDERING that he met him only once and that the meeting took place twenty-four years ago, Herbert Sitwell remembers Leon Tolbert with an eerie exactitude.

"I remember the shoes he was wearing," Sitwell says. "I remember his *socks*."

Twenty-four years ago Herbert Sitwell was chairman of the English department at Evergreen University, a small liberal arts college on the outskirts of Chicago. A mainstay of the department had recently died—Mrs. Miriam Minsky, who taught Greek tragedy and a popular survey course called Embarrassing Moments in Modern Literature. In this course she discussed Faulkner as an embarrassing drunk, Hemingway as an embarrassing drunk, Ezra Pound as just generally embarrassing. Sitwell was not looking to replace Mrs. Minsky but rather to begin anew with a different sort of instructor, one who was thoroughly schooled in the fundamentals of classical literature and modern poetry and who—this was especially important—was alive. To this end he interviewed almost anybody who was willing to spend some time talking to him. One day that was exactly what Leon Tolbert did.

From the moment he stepped into Sitwell's office, Tolbert distinguished himself from the other candidates vying for

Mrs. Minsky's position. He was alone among them all, for instance, in refusing to send in his résumé.

"I *am* my vitae!" he declared on the telephone. "I will not be diminished to a few words and dates on a piece of cheap white onionskin paper!"

The secretary who spoke to Tolbert scheduled him for an appointment with Chairman Sitwell because she was frightened by Tolbert, who she says reminded her of a maniacal office supply salesman who had once stalked her for weeks in pursuit of an order for ballpoint pens.

So even before Tolbert entered Sitwell's office he had been singled out as different from the rest, unique, fresh blood.

"I'd notified security before he arrived," Sitwell says. "Just in case. You never know."

Tolbert was more than punctual. His appointment was at three, and he was there at one-thirty. He sat in the anteroom outside the chairman's office, his briefcase on his lap and his hands folded on top of the briefcase, not moving, appearing not even to blink, for an entire hour and a half. This served only to increase the secretary's level of fear until, at five minutes before three, she ran screaming from the room.

Herbert Sitwell remembers the limp and the painful grimace on Tolbert's face as Leon rose to meet him.

"The OED," Tolbert said by way of explanation. "Dropped it on my toe last night."[1]

During the first few minutes of the interview, Sitwell talked casually about the weather, as he did with all the applicants.

---

1. *The origin of this alibi is unknown, but it could well be that Tolbert himself created it. Since then, wimpy English instructors all over the country have been known to use this excuse when bowing out of sporting activities in which they saw no hope of competing.*

"More humid than usual this time of year," he would say. Or "It should rain soon."

Tolbert was not one to play the empty banter game, however. "Do you know how many times the weather is mentioned, on average, in each of Shakespeare's plays?" he asked.

"No," Sitwell said.

"Don't you want to guess?"

"Well, not really," Sitwell said.

"Oh, come on."

"I wouldn't have any idea."

"Pretty please. Just give me a wild guess."

"All right. Ten."

"Ten? I did say *all* the plays, didn't I? Comedies, tragedies, histories, everything. That includes *Timon of Athens*."

"Fifteen?" hazarded Sitwell. "Twenty?"

"Try thirty-three. And that's just on average. In *The Tempest* alone the weather is mentioned fifty-three times, and in *King Lear*, sixty."

"Fascinating," Sitwell said. "Where'd you come up with these numbers?"

"I counted," Tolbert said.

"Oh, come on, you couldn't have counted every—"

"But I did. I counted the number of times the weather was mentioned in each of his plays. I included weather-related references as well, such as when Hamlet is pointing out the shapes of clouds to Polonius. That's borderline, I admit it, but I felt—"

"You went through every play page by page and—"

"Years ago," Tolbert said. "The summer just flew by."

Sitwell nodded, then smiled dimly. He felt oddly unmoored, as if suddenly in a strange place in which he was sure of nothing. "Well, then," he said, "let's talk about this job. Miss Plumsworthy, my secretary, told me you refused to send in a résumé or references. Why?"

"I feel as though I represent myself better than lifeless, bloodless words on a scrap of onionskin paper."

"Onionskin?"

"That's right."

"Onionskin probably wouldn't be appropriate for a résumé, Mr. Tolbert."

"My point exactly."

"I beg your pardon. I think I missed something."

Tolbert smiled mysteriously.

Sitwell cleared his throat. "In that case," he said, "tell me about yourself. Where'd you receive your education?"

Tolbert's smile broadened. "In space and time, Mr. Sitwell. Wisdom, patience, love, and the great dead white men and women we all so revere have been my teachers. You?"

"Colgate," he said.

"Ah."

"So I'm to understand you have no formal education?"

"Do I have a degree, you mean? A fancy piece of onionskin paper with the name of some super-duper university scrawled all over it to impress you with? No."[2]

"You're determined *not* to impress me, is that it?"

---

[2]. Tolbert's obsession with onionskin dates back to his earliest memories. His father insisted he use onionskin for everything, from crayon pictures to his unfinished novel. During one particularly bleak winter when a snowstorm trapped the family inside the house for a week, the only item they ran out of was toilet paper. Leon's father, however, had a solution. . . .

"On the contrary, I will impress you. But if you need a piece of onionskin—"

"Fine, fine. Where were we?"

"I'm here to be interviewed for the position Mrs. Minsky left in the wake of her . . . of her . . ."

"Death was the culprit, I believe."

"Ah, yes. Death. 'The green-eyed monster which doth mock the meat it feeds on.'"

"I think you mean envy."

"One doesn't die of envy, Mr. Sitwell. One dies of cancer, heart disease, emphysema, the plague, but not—"

"Envy is 'the green-eyed monster which doth mock the meat it feeds on,' Mr. Tolbert. *Othello*, Act something or other. You ought to know that. At least I would certainly think so. I mean, for goodness' sake, man, you've counted every mention of the weather in Shakespeare's plays. I should think you'd know the most—"

"Frankly," Tolbert said, "I feel as though I'm your guy. I feel as though I have what it takes to do what needs to be done for Wintergreen University. I know just about everything, to tell you the truth."

"Do you know that you're interviewing for a job at *Evergreen* University?"

"Well, I know *something* about everything, anyway."

"Is that so?" Sitwell almost laughed. "I think that's the first time anyone's ever told me that."

"This is the first time you've met Leon Tolbert."

"So it is. Mind if I test you, Mr. Tolbert? A little quiz?"

"Not at all."

"Tell me something about—oh, Edith Wharton."

"Well, for starters, she, like Mrs. Minsky, is dead."

If Sitwell found this last remark to be even the least bit amusing, the expression on his face gave no indication of such. "Continue," he said.

"She's also one of those novelists many of us leave behind in high school, which is too bad, because she was an extraordinary writer and a fascinating woman, though you might never know this if all you took into consideration was her name. I mean *Edith Wharton* does not exactly conjure up an image of literary grace. What it conjures up is an image of the lady next door, the one who's constantly complaining that your music's too loud. Likewise, *Ethan Frome* doesn't exactly sound like something you'd want to cuddle up with in front of a fire, but it's a brilliant novel, as is *The Age of Innocence*."

"Interesting," Sitwell said. "But I was hoping for something a bit more provocative."

"Well, she *was* one of the first people Henry James knew who owned a car," Tolbert said, "and the two of them would

often go on long rides together through the beautiful countryside, arguing the relative merits of the third-person omni-
scient narrator. And despite the fact that she lived through
the end of the Victorian era and wore those big hats and long
dresses—and yes, carried a parasol—Edith Wharton *did* have
an extremely satisfactory love affair with Morgan Fullerton."

"Morgan Fullerton? I've never heard of him."

"And judging from his name, you probably never will
again. . . . That was a joke, Mr. Sitwell."

"Hmmm."

CHAPTER 2

T HE CROWD BEGAN to swell. Members of the campus pep band, who had been practicing outside the music building, were drifting over to see what all the commotion was about. A couple of local high school kids, skipping classes for the day, were urging Tolbert to jump. And Maynard O'Neill, director of nonhuman resources, wanted to know if the professor had obtained a permit to give a lecture from an oak tree.

O'Neill read from a manual of campus ordinances: "'Section eighteen, subparagraph three-A. No member of the faculty or staff shall engage in instruction from any pulpit, dais, or otherwise conforming auditorial dispersion facility located outside of an approved university classroom without first obtaining, in writing, a permit indicating he or she has been authorized to do so.' Do you have a permit, Professor?"

At which point a crumpled up sheet of paper descended from the tree like a withered leaf.

O'Neill examined it:

TODAY'S QUIZ Match the writer (Column A) with the actor or actress (Column B) who you think would be a TV producer's first choice to portray him or her in a miniseries.

A	B
F. Scott Fitzgerald	Tony Danza
Richard Wright	Karen Valentine
George Sand	Hal Linden
Theodore Dreiser	Barbara Eden
Kate Chopin	Farrah Fawcett
Harriet Beecher Stowe	Linda Gray
George Eliot	Tom Selleck
Daphne du Maurier	Carol Burnett
Joyce Carol Oates	Mr. T
James Fenimore Cooper	Elizabeth Montgomery
Sylvia Plath	John Ritter
Fyodor Dostoyevsky	Diahann Carroll
Jack Kerouac	Melissa Gilbert
Jane Austen	Gavin McLeod
Ford Madox Ford	Lindsay Wagner
Edmund Spenser	Valerie Bertinelli
Emily Brontë	Susan Lucci
Marianne Moore	Patrick Duffy
Zora Neale Hurston	Gregory Harrison
Emile Zola	Loni Anderson
Anaïs Nin	Robert Guillaume

"This isn't what I had in mind," Maynard O'Neill said, frowning.

Taller than the average American poet, E. E. Cummings—or rather e. e. cummings—wrote some of our smallest and most circuitous poems. Reading them is like taking a new path through the forest or falling down a hill—it's a physical experience. It's also fun: cummings—or rather Cummings (he preferred the lower case only through the thirties)—liked slang and jazz, and he put it all in his poems. His first book of poetry was published by his mother. It's what we wish our mother would do. We have lots of little poems around here somewhere, and we think they're good enough to be published, if she'll pay for it, that is.

—L.T., MARCH 3, 1993

CHAPTER 30

LENNY BRUCE—UNPLUGGED.

"ANYTHING ELSE?"

"Yes, there *is* something else." Herbert Sitwell shuffled some papers on his desk, cleared his throat, and looked Tolbert straight in the eye. "What can you tell me about Lenny Bruce? I saw him on television once, and in my opinion—"

"Well, funny you should bring him up," Tolbert said, "because I've been thinking about him lately. Or not him, really, but the fact that while almost everybody has heard *of* Lenny Bruce, only a small fraction of those people have ever actually *heard* him. Live, I mean, or even on TV or the radio. His act, in other words. And, you know, I think this is an example of a pretty dreadful trend, one which I see slowly developing before our very eyes: the same thing that's happened to poets and writers is going to happen to comedians, to singers, even to movie stars—we're all going to know their names, but nobody's going to have heard or seen their stuff! Nobody reads anymore, right? It's just too hard. Well, you know what, Mr. Sitwell, soon *it will become too hard to listen to a radio or even to watch TV!* We won't even be couch potatoes. We'll just be potatoes! Lying there on the ground. Our faces drooling in the—"

"I asked you about Lenny Bruce, Mr. Tolbert, and you've commenced with a piece of social commentary centered around—"

"Something unexpected," Tolbert said. "Perhaps that's in my favor, though? I mean, anyone can talk about Lenny Bruce—his politics, that is, or his language or the effect he's had on other comedians, et cetera. But to talk about Lenny

Bruce while not talking about Lenny Bruce . . . One of my real talents is indirection. The look-away pass. Saying I'm doing one thing while I do precisely another. Perhaps this is the particular sort of teacher Evergreen is looking for."

Yes, and perhaps we might hire a two-headed monkey as chancellor, Sitwell thought. But there was something about Tolbert that fascinated him. He was clearly well read, and it was evident that he did have a large capacity for trivia. It would be a shame if his peculiar talents were lost on the world. This could happen, Sitwell knew: he'd had an uncle not unlike Tolbert. Uncle Henry. King of the Arcane, they used to call him. He, too, had tried to put his talents to use, but he was laughed at, ridiculed, made the butt of jokes. He became a lawn maintenance supervisor and died in his sleep at the age of thirty-seven. The same could happen to Tolbert. As he stared at the strange young man a vision of Uncle Henry rose before him, and suddenly tears welled up in Sitwell's eyes.

"Are you all right, Mr. Sitwell?"

"I'm fine. Thank you. Allergies, they're driving me batty."

"Of course. You know they drove John Donne batty, too. And Sir Walter Scott as well. Do you realize how many times—"

"I have a proposition for you, Mr. Tolbert."

"Which is?"

"Regarding Mrs. Minsky's position . . ."

"Yes?"

"I'm afraid you're not what we're looking for."

"Oh," Leon said, visibly deflating before Sitwell's eyes. And at this point Sitwell saw him, briefly, wearing a light green jumpsuit and a baseball hat, holding a broken sprinkler in one hand and a bag of fertilizer in the other.

"There is another spot in the English department, however—it just opened up—and I think you'd be . . . well, I think it's something you might be able to do."

Suddenly Leon revived. "Of course," he said, leaning forward a bit. "In the English department! Anything in the English department would be welcome indeed!"

Sitwell pursed his lips, then nodded. "Well, as you may know, Mr. Tolbert, many students come to us not fully prepared to assume the normal workload of a college freshman. Frankly, many of them are illiterate. Why do we let them matriculate? God only knows, but if we sent them all away, we'd be the smallest college on the continent. At any rate, we do our best to teach them a few of the skills they'll need before going on to some of the richer aspects of a college education. And that's where you come in."

Tolbert said nothing. His eyes were trained on Sitwell's mouth.

"Your erudition is just what these kids could use," Sitwell said. "I want you to break them in. I want you to take them and turn them into the seekers of knowledge they were meant to be."

Tolbert's head was now cocked to one side. He clearly didn't get what Sitwell was driving at, but the mystery was about to end.

"I want you to teach remedial English," Sitwell said. "Nothing fancy. Just the basics. How to use a pen and pencil. What a vowel is. That sort of thing."

Looking back today, Herbert Sitwell thinks he was perhaps

overly fond of his uncle Henry. What could he have been thinking when he offered Tolbert a job? It wasn't his responsibility to save him from a life of yard work. And yet this was what he'd done—he had led Leon Tolbert onto an academic treadmill from which it would take him more than twenty years to dismount.

CHAPTER 3.

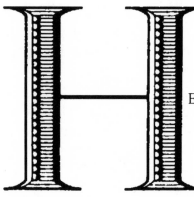ELLO, LEON."

"Is that you, Dorothea?"

"It is."

"What are you doing here?"

"What am *I* doing here? The question, Leon—the question on my mind and I'm sure on everybody's mind—is what are *you* doing *there*?"

"Don't change the subject."

"I'm not."

"Are too."

"Leon, *please* . . ."

Tolbert's students, sensing that class was over, slowly began to drift away. "I didn't know he was married," Mrs. Tolbert heard one say to another.

"I always thought—"

"Me too."

"Well, thank you, Dorothea," Leon said. "Thank you for disrupting my class."

"You are conducting your class from a sagging branch, Leon!"

"I know that! You don't think I know that? I know that!"

"Leon," she said. "Why?"

A long silence followed. A leaf fell to the ground, then a pencil.

"Why," he said sort of softly. "Why. Leave it to you to ask why."

"People are worried about you," she said. "Can't you tell?"

BLAKE'S DICTA: "YOU NEVER KNOW WHAT IS ENOUGH UNTIL
YOU KNOW WHAT IS MORE THAN ENOUGH."

She was looking straight up—not easy on her neck. All she
could see was Leon's shoe. She turned her head a bit to the
right and was able to see his hands, his necktie, and finally
his small-eyed face, looking down at her. "People are starting
to wonder."

"Wonder what?"

"You know."

"I see," he said. "I've assumed Blakean dimensions, have I?
I've become a kind of wild and wondrous literary personage.
My flights of fancy confuse and bewilder them, as they've not
yet opened their minds to the beauty and the glory of God's
creation."

"They think you're a crackpot."

"That was my next guess," he said.

Mrs. Tolbert stood staring up at her husband, who didn't
look as though he was making his way down. In fact he

seemed to be making himself more comfortable, moving from one branch to another in search of a firmer hold. As he did so, some of his papers fluttered down to her.

"Leon," she said, "get out of the tree."

"It's very nice up here," he said.

"I'm sure it is," she said, "but we don't have to live in trees anymore. We have a house."

"This is not what I had in mind, Dorrie," he said then.

"Excuse me?"

"All of this. I'd meant to be more than just a remedial English instructor. I think it's time we returned to Pelham. Just for the summer. A little R-and-R. And I can work on the book."

"That's a wonderful idea, Leon."

"Things blow over," he said, ripping his trousers as he began to descend from the tree. "Everybody'll forget my little episodes by next year. Next year it will be quite different. I'm really looking forward to next year."

"Yes, dear," she said, taking his hand as he jumped.

"Arizona's beautiful, isn't it?" he said.

"It is."

"We like it here."

"We do."

"Very much."

They walked toward his office arm in arm.

"I'm not even gone yet, and already I can't wait to get back," he said. "Isn't that funny?"

"That is."

Many years ago, when we were burning with a hard gemlike flame, we disdained and ridiculed our parents. We did not look forward to adulthood at all.

Having since become adults ourselves, however, we would like to weigh in here with a total across-the-board condemnation of this entire age and its values and anybody who is happy with it, especially the kids, who disdain and ridicule us every chance they get.

That being said, allow us to move on: literary pranks. We used to love them. While our friends were out shooting marbles or playing basketball, we, the literary-minded, were at home in the basement, calling rare-book stores with a variation on the Prince-Albert-in-a-can routine.

C H A P T E R 3

"Do you have Shakespeare in a quarto?" we'd inquire.
"Yes."
"Well, you'd probably get a good price on it at auction!"
The shopkeeper would hang up, and we'd roar with laughter.

Another one of our favorites was to pretend we were related to people whom we weren't. When the doorbell rang, for instance, and our parents weren't there, we'd crack the door a bit and very gruffly mumble, "Yes?" And if the voice outside asked for, say, our father, we'd shout, "Our father! Our father! Our father is George Bernard Shaw, for goodness' sake!" or something to that effect.

It was very amusing, as you can imagine.

Of course, as we became older, some of our pranks became more complex. Once, while we were studying overseas, we left a pair of crab claws on Anthony Hecht's doorstep. That kept us laughing for days! Later we embarked on the traditional dig-up-the-poet *rite of passage. A frightening event. We dug up Robert Browning and put him back a week later. These days, kids wouldn't know a good dead poet if they fell into a hole with one—which was exactly what happened to us!*

—L.T., APRIL 2, 1993

AD HERBERT Sitwell known the path he was sending Leon Tolbert down, it is certain he would have reconsidered.

"I reconsidered moments after hiring him," he has said. "Then again moments after that. But it was too late. The wheels had already started turning. Kismet had been enjoined. Fate had been invited to Leon Tolbert's party, and I was the doorman. You know, I still can't apologize enough to everybody. I'm so sorry."

Ironically, neither Evergreen University nor Herbert Sitwell himself suffered much from Tolbert's short stay there. Although records are sketchy, it appears that for the greater part of the single semester he taught at Evergreen, Tolbert actually taught what he'd been hired to teach—remedial English—and with some proficiency, according to one former student, Ken Calley, now a sportscaster in Des Moines, Iowa. "He was the greatest," Ken says. "Superior, top-notch, numero uno. Toward the end of the semester, things got a bit interesting, of course. But that was fine. He saw daylight, so he took off down the field."

Interesting, in that Tolbert began to drift from the required text, although "drift" may not be the appropriate word, as it presumes Tolbert himself wasn't in control.

"I want to thank Jimmy Nowell for bringing in an example of our word for the day," Tolbert told his class. "Was it hard to find an example of the word 'toaster,' Jimmy? No? Good!

It was right there, on the side of the toaster? That's terrific, Jimmy. Good detective work. You know, class, there are other places you might find words. For example, you might find them in a book, and you know what? I just happened to bring one in with me—a book, that is . . . I left my toaster at home! Anyhow, I brought in a novel—lots of pages, see, lots of specks on the white paper. And I'll bet the word 'toaster' is in here somewhere. Could be. Hey, I've got an idea! Why don't I just read the novel aloud, and when I come to the word 'toaster,' somebody stop me."

But it turned out that not once in *Finnegans Wake* does Joyce mention a toaster. By the time Tolbert had finished reading it, however, the semester was over, as was his tenure at Evergreen: only hours after the school's commencement ceremonies had ended, Tolbert submitted a letter of resignation to Herbert Sitwell, claiming that he had been "duped into teaching dopes."

"Leon didn't know what he was doing," his wife, Dorothea, recollects. "He lived in the clouds. He was lucky to get dressed every morning, much less find his way to work. He was crazy to quit."

But Tolbert's craziness no doubt helped him secure his next teaching position, at Cordell Union, a prep school for boys interested in athletics and little else. Herbert Sitwell was so happy that Tolbert had quit—and that he hadn't had to fire him—that he actually gave Tolbert a favorable job-performance rating. About Tolbert's teaching ability, Sitwell wrote the following, ellipses and all: "Leon Tolbert may be the last . . . of a certain kind of instructor. His . . . technique and . . . methods are without compare. Et cetera!"

CHAPTER 33

ENGLISH 312—*The Hidden Aesthetic: An Enlightened Approach to Understanding Almost Anything.* Instructor: Leon Tolbert. An informal roundtable discussion held weekly at the professor's house. Thursday 10:00 A.M. Bring your own lunch.

By the middle of his last semester at NACC Tolbert's courses had taken on the air of a kind of brilliant literary floor show, with the increasingly despondent professor in the role of master of ceremonies. Able somehow to balance his training as an English instructor on the one hand and his encroaching madness on the other, Tolbert developed his most ambitious course offering yet. Entitled The Hidden Aesthetic: An Enlightened Approach to Understanding Almost Anything, it saw the professor no longer limiting himself to discussions of literature and literary personalities; suddenly the world opened wide for him, and to the chagrin of his students, his colleagues, and the administration, he lectured not only on poetry and drama but also on modern dance, classical music, birds, magic, psychology, and science fiction, sometimes all on the same day. He would also occasionally talk about his health problems and his wife's inability to, in the professor's words, "tell the difference between a teapot and a tire iron." At the end of that semester the students gathered for what would be Tolbert's final final exam. It consisted of one question: "Describe the universe and give three examples." Sadly for most of his students, there was no extra-credit section.

Did William Shakespeare write Macbeth *or did Christopher Marlowe? Here in Flagstaff, as elsewhere, there's been an ongoing battle over the true identity of the author of Shakespeare's plays. Not a physical, bloodletting battle, but a battle of words, which, believe it or not, do hurt almost as much as sticks and bones, depending on their size (and a couple of the pointy-heads in this department know some pretty big words). Anyhow, the theory most folks buy now is that while Shakespeare himself wrote* The Tempest, Much Ado About Nothing, *and* Romeo and Juliet, *Christopher Marlowe wrote* Macbeth, *Sir Francis Bacon wrote* A Midsummer Night's Dream, *and Lee Harvey Oswald wrote the* The Merchant of Venice. *Experts have long suspected Bacon's hand in*

C H A P T E R 34

at least of one of Shakespeare's plays, and Marlowe made no secret of his desire to get credit for his work on Macbeth, *but what led to Oswald's involvement with* The Merchant of Venice? *No one's quite sure, but the evidence is compelling: Shakespeare's signature on a long-lost motion picture contract, wherein the bard was paid seven shillings for the rights to his life story, the highlight of which was his 1589 confession to the Warren Commission.*

—L.T., MARCH 26, 1993

IF YOU ENJOYED READING EZRA POUND'S CANTOS, WAIT
UNTIL YOU SEE HASBRO'S NEW EZRA POUND CUDDLY DOLL.

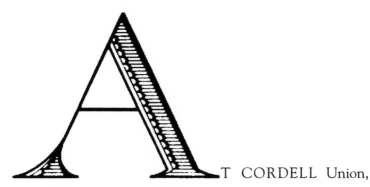T CORDELL Union, Leon Tolbert wasted little time in getting away from what he was hired to do.

"Most great writers become great by breaking the rules they want me to teach you," he said to his class on the first day they gathered. "So whaddaya say we skip the remedial part and get right down to the English?"

And get right down to it he did. In that first semester he discoursed on subjects ranging from Ezra Pound to Jim Thompson, from William Shakespeare to Flannery O'Connor, from Jane Austen to Jerry Lewis—in no particular order and for no particular reason. Most of his lectures were brief, some barely touching upon their intended topics, but what truly distinguished Leon Tolbert's remedial English classes was that Leon Tolbert made it a rule never to mention remedial English.

Remarkably, his tenure at Cordell Union was quite successful; semester after semester he received as high a performance rating as was possible. But Tolbert's wife remembers him worrying about his position.

"He always thought somebody, somewhere, was going to catch on. But they never did, at least not at Cordell. And eventually Leon didn't care anymore. The kids there loved him, and that was all that mattered."

Tolbert's popularity at Cordell might have had to do with the nature of the institution itself, however, and the particular scheduling of all his classes: directly after gym. Most of his students were still showering when his class ended, and if they arrived at all, many took the opportunity to sleep through it.

CHAPTER

EXCERPTS FROM

MR. NABOKOV'S NEIGHBORHOOD

A WORK IN PROGRESS

BY LEON TOLBERT

1. INTRODUCTION

Our trek to your lap (or your desk or wherever we might be resting right now) began over fifty years ago, in a beachfront cottage on the coast of Maine.

Maine! What a fine state to visit, very briefly, as we did one summer when we were quite young. Our parents had rented a small house just north of Bar Harbor, not far from the Canadian border. We had a feeling something was going to be different that summer. And something was indeed different, monumentally so. For not long after we arrived did we learn that staying in a cottage just a few doors down from us were—amazingly—William Faulkner, Dorothy Parker, W. H. Auden, E. B. White, and, we were told, the ghost of Harley Granville-Barker, English critic, dramatist, director, and actor, then only recently deceased, lately becoming more so.

We were, as we said, quite young at the time, but our parents had taught us well, and thus we were far from unacquainted with the works of these mighty minds. In fact our bedtime reading frequently consisted of excerpts from *The*

Sound and the Fury, a title which we understood to be *The Sound of the Furry*, and so for months kept waiting, on our way to sleep, for the furry thing, whatever it was, to make a noise. And yet it never did.

At any rate, it was not without a bit of trepidation that we introduced ourselves to these seminal figures one rainy morning shortly after we arrived. Prepared to be sent away with an autographed napkin or perhaps a few poetic sentiments scribbled on the back of an envelope, we were pleasantly surprised to be welcomed as a "harmless diversion" by them all and then later allowed to visit each morning when they were supposed to be working but were often just waking up.

Anyhow, rather suddenly and inexplicably, our parents departed for Europe on a cruise ship, leaving us to care for ourselves, whereupon we seized the opportunity to show up, blankets in hand and tears in our eyes, on the doorstep of our literary friends. To their great credit, they took us in, giving us a room overlooking the water and teaching us immediately how to make whiskey sours, clean ashtrays, and find their mysteriously disappearing shoes—the work, no doubt, of the mischievous Harley Granville-Barker, English critic, dramatist, director, and actor, now a learned beach house poltergeist, making life for us rather unpredictable, to say the least!

And so the summer passed, with untold numbers of amusing incidents taking place, such as one might expect when one considered the company we were keeping. Faulkner would say something, you know, in his way, and then Parker in hers, and then Auden would say something very much in his, and so on—they were at once very droll and thought-provoking, and sometimes rather silly. Auden and Faulkner even collaborated on several short projects, two of which were later published pseudonymously, the fictitious author's name actually a diverting anagram of their own. And one night Dorothy Parker did something none of us thought was humanly possible. And yet there she was, doing it!

Well, our parents eventually returned, and we drove back with them to Long Island, never to see any of the writers (or that ghost) again. And this, in a misleading, meandering way, brings us to the point of the work you're now holding.

We hope you enjoy it!

Paris, Trieste, Flagstaff, 1992

2. SIX *LARGELY* LITERARY LECTURES

I. NATHANIEL HAWTHORNE What does it take to be a great writer? A great mind, yes, a gentle spirit, of course—and, some say, a large bristling mustache. Nathaniel Hawthorne had all three. Like Mark Twain and others before and since, Hawthorne had a great big mustache, which he used in all sorts of ways as he wrote *The Scarlet Letter*, *The House of the Seven Gables*, and his other fine novels. Food sometimes became lodged in his mustache, and instead of having to get up and get something to eat, Hawthorne would simply rummage through the hair on his upper lip. When he came to a difficult passage and had to stop and think, he often stroked his mustache, much as if it were a dog or a cat, the only difference being his mustache didn't drool or purr. Rubbing it would help him come up with the next word, and off he would go. It would not be taking things too far to say that to a writer like Hawthorne, a large bristly mustache is a kind of muse and certainly the sine qua non of first-rate allegory; thus without it, one can say with almost complete confidence, *The Scarlet Letter* might never have been written.

II. FRÉDÉRIC CHOPIN Since Chopin's time, the term "romantic" has gone through something of a sea change. These days a romantic lad takes his girl to a secluded cavern just outside of town, where he's secretly assembled a candlelit dinner for two, a violinist, and a dancing bear for her entertainment. In the mid-nineteenth century, however, "romantic" meant writing something beautiful and then dying, usually of tuberculosis. Chopin was only thirty-nine when he died, Keats was twenty-six: both are hailed as Romantics. Even though he lived longer, Chopin is considered the archetype of the consumptive Romantic artist. Before him, mazurkas and polonaises were to the nineteenth century what square-dance music is to ours: Chopin—half Polish, half French—turned them into something serious. His last years were marked by a torrid affair with

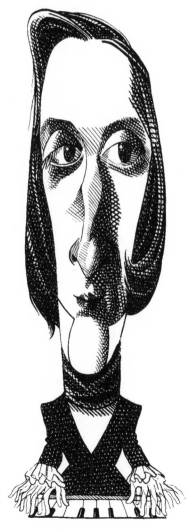

the novelist George Sand, which—who knows?—may have hastened his death or lengthened his life. Anyway, it's good to know even Romantics can have a fling every now and then.

III. DOROTHY L. SAYERS It's not our job to present refresher courses in detective fiction, but as long as we're here, we might as well point out some of its basic tenets.

You've got your good-guy P.I.'s on the one hand and your bad-guy crooks on the other. And of the good-guy P.I.'s—the private dicks, we mean—there's the hard-boiled kind and soft-boiled kind. And of the soft-boiled kind, they don't come much softer than Lord Peter Wimsey, served sunny-side up in more Dorothy L. Sayers novels than we can count.

Peter Wimsey.

With a name like that, we'd rather expect him to be soft-boiled, wouldn't we? "Rather expect" is something a soft-boiled detective might say. "Hands off the dame, Wimsey," is not exactly the sort of dialogue one stumbles across in a Dorothy L. Sayers novel. How would we take it if someone called us soft-boiled? We're not sure, but it wouldn't bother Lord Peter Wimsey in the least. In fact, he'd rather expect it.

IV. JANE AUSTEN We were once surprised to learn that people other than ourselves like to read Jane Austen.

"Surprised" may not be the right word: we were astounded. We'd found a book by her, *Mansfield Park*, on a shelf in the basement, read it, loved it, and felt we'd made a great discovery. She was our secret: Austen and us, we were kind of a team there for a while. And yet when we casually mentioned her name at one of the soirees we attend almost nightly, not only did we find the room filled with Austen admirers, we also learned that she is generally regarded as one of the greatest nov-

elists of the nineteenth century. After which our interest in her faded a bit. Hard to say why, exactly, but it's just not the same anymore. There was a time, however brief, when Jane was ours and ours alone; now she belongs to the world.

V. ANSEL ADAMS Not only was Ansel Adams a brilliant photographer, he played a pretty mean piano as well. We know this because our niece, Monica, actually played a duet with him at a recital in San Diego just two years before he died. They were so cute up there on the stage together, Mr. Adams and Monica!

"Play 'Chopsticks,'" someone in the audience shouted.

"All right," Mr. Adams said. "'Chopsticks' it is." Whereupon he and Monica broke into a rousing rendition of the keyboard classic.

"'Three Blind Mice,'" someone's mother cried out when they had finished. "Real fast!"

"Your wish is our command," Mr. Adams said, and indeed it was. They didn't miss a single note!

The two finished their performance with a delightful version of "Row, Row, Row Your Boat," in which the audience was asked to participate while Mr. Adams took pictures.

Unfortunately, they came out blurred.

VI. WILLIAM BUTLER YEATS Not everything we tell you is true. We make some of it up. What we said about Ansel Adams, for instance, isn't true. For the most part, at least. And what we said about Hawthorne—a total fabrication. So there's no reason to believe us when we tell you that William Butler Yeats, the great Irish bowler, wrote brilliant poetry in his spare time. No reason to believe us when we write, as we are about to, that Yeats's work was characterized not simply by its artful integration of image and idea but

also by its lyrical realism, its precision, and its economy— qualities not often associated with an indoor sport.

3. AUTHOR'S NOTE

Those of you thumbing through these pages for the first time may be interested in finding out how we decide on whom to include. Why Virginia Woolf and not, say, her husband Leonard? Why Richard Wagner, the composer, and not Robert Wagner, the actor?

Well, the decision-making process is long and tedious, with the first requirement being fame. (If fame were not a requirement we would probably be including you.)

At our office here in Flagstaff there is a room in which the names of all famous people are kept in a confidential file.

Believe it or not, there are more than 28,600 legitimately famous people, including people like Tori Spelling and Kahlil Gibran. Our second requirement—that you must be talented—excludes them, however.

That still leaves more than 10,000 people.

Of those, we can eliminate half, because as famous as they might be, we've never heard of them. And we can throw out half of the rest because we remember reading a boring poem by them in high school.

And this is where the selection process begins in earnest. A list of the 2,500 remaining famous people is now distributed to a committee on which every conceivable socioeconomic group or subgroup is represented. Several times a year this committee gathers for a working weekend in a parking garage just outside Dothan, Alabama. Meanwhile, back at our office in Flagstaff, two receptionists are idly picking out of a hat the names of the famous people who are featured in this work.

4. GLOSSARY OF TERMS

Blurb: A fawning sentence found somewhere on the back cover of a book. Blurbs are generally written by "recognized authorities," many of whom so excel at writing blurbs that blurb-writing is now all they have time to do. It begins innocently enough. The blurb-writer composes an honest tribute to a book he's enjoyed, such as: "Brace yourself. This book will shake you up, throw you down, knock you out, and make you cry. And that's just the first page." Soon other authors, agents, and publishers are sending him additional books for one of his "honest tributes." He naively complies. "Get ready," he writes. "This is no ordinary novel. The characters in it are so real I think some of them are living with me right now. Which is fine. I just wish they'd pick up after themselves!" He soon finds that work on his own book starts to slow; no longer is he able to capture the spirit that once propelled his narrative. Besides, a book takes years to write, a blurb takes only a few minutes! He begins to see blurb-writing as a separate art form—incisive, distinct, independent of any reference. The book becomes the vehicle for the blurb. No longer is it even necessary for him to read the book before he writes his glowing tribute. "Warning to the reader," he declares. "Do not go gentle into this good novel." And on yet another tome: "Watch out! This baby will rip your heart right out of your chest, then show it to you, still beating, while you scream in horror and—yes—delight."

Creative Writing: A knack for turning insipid fantasies into a college course credit.

Dibs: A claim on something, as in "I've got dibs on the liver." Which reminds us, there was this guy at a camp we attended when we were young, and he would always get dibs on the rolls by licking his index finger and touching them. We were only supposed to get one roll each, but this guy, Marvin Schorsky, well, he would lick his finger and touch three of them, one after another, saying, "This one's mine, this one's mine, this one's mine." God, how we hated him! Finally, after he'd been doing this for about a week, he did it again—he licked his finger and said, "This one's mine, this one's mine, this one's mine." So we chewed up a piece of hamburger until it was nice and gooey, then spit it into the palm of our hand and smeared it over all three rolls. "There," we said, "you can have it, you can have it, you can have it." If you're wondering what any of this has to do with literature, see Fun.

Free verse: Poetry lacking in regular meter, rhyme, or line length. Free verse is sometimes confused with two-for-one verse and scratch-and-dent verse, the latter of which can be had for a song.

Fun: A sensation of enjoyment, often intensified when experienced in the presence of relatives. Fun is usually divided into three generation-specific categories. For parents, there's "good clean fun," which includes playing catch, going to an amusement park, and completing an entire game of Scrabble without cheating; for grandparents, there's "old-fashioned fun," which includes all of the above and then making five pounds of salt-water taffy; and for grandchildren, there's "real honest-to-God fun," which includes gluing together the pages of your father's new *Playboy*, slipping a dead raccoon into your brother's bed, and flushing all the toilets while your sister's taking a shower. The relationship between fun and literature has been the subject of countless studies.

Immelmann turn: A maneuver in which an airplane first completes half a loop then half a roll in order to simultaneously gain altitude and change direction in flight, named after the German aviator Max Immelmann. The term is also applied to writers who are capable of similar maneuvers within a single sentence. Faulkner is perhaps best known for his

Immelmanns in *Absalom, Absalom!* Very few writers can successfully sustain a series of Immelmanns. When an Immelmann is attempted, and the writer fails, as did Thomas Mann throughout his career, the result is known as Die Opus Floppus.

Meaning: Dante believed there are four levels of meaning: the literal, the allegorical, the moral, and the anagogical. Others believe that a fifth level, and perhaps even a screened-in porch out back, should be added. Lately there's been a rash of books that have successfully eluded all types of meaning, except, of course, a financial one. See Dibs.

Metaphor: The equating of one thing with another seemingly unrelated thing, usually to suggest some relationship between the two. For example, in Delmore Schwartz's "The Heavy Bear That Goes With Me," the "bear" is in fact the narrator's own body, and the substitution of "bear" for "body," within the context of the poem, serves to reify the conflict between the narrator's spiritual self and his physical self. Of course metaphor is often misinterpreted, and it could be argued that Schwartz was simply referring to the large brown grizzly that used to follow him to work every morning.

Negative capability: The extent to which an editor feels compelled to publish serious literature rather than best-selling fiction.

Novel: A story that could stand to be shorter.

Novella: Like a novel, but less so.

Novellina: A literary doll made by Kenner. When you wind Novellina up and lend her twenty dollars, she dumps her high school sweetheart, hangs out all night at an espresso bar, and complains constantly about the amorous overtures of her English professor.

Obscurity: A subdivision in West Los Angeles. In Obscurity, many an aspiring screenwriter lives in the sewers and waits patiently beneath the street grating for a pair of shoes to pass by so that he might lick their tasty soles.

Picaresque: A type of fiction, usually a novel, comprising a series of satiric episodes or sketches. The best-known picaresque novels are probably *Don Quixote*, *Tristram Shandy*, and *Tom Jones*, all of which were written in or before the eighteenth century and all of which, by virtue of their inordinate length, would seem to suggest that the relative popularity of the picaresque novel is inversely proportional to the number of people who've actually read one.

Poetic license: A document issued to Walt Whitman two months before he wrote "Song of Myself."

Prolepsis: A figure of speech in which an anticipated event is referred to as though it had already happened. For instance, when Hamlet, wounded, says, "Horatio, I am dead," he is not actually dead, but simply hinting to the audience that he has, in the past, felt better. Likewise, in Frederick Waddle's quartet about fraternity life in the seventies, *The Naked Fellas*, prolepsis is used to great effect when Jeffrey, who has been caught cheating on a chemistry exam, says, "I'm dead," prior to actually dying.

Pseudonym: A fictitious name assumed by an author. Pseudonyms are used for various reasons. Women writers used them when it was not considered ladylike for women to write. George Eliot was the pseudonym for Mary Ann Evans, for instance, and the Brontë sisters created an entire pseudonymous family—Currer (Charlotte), Ellis (Emily), and Acton (Anne) Bell, pseudonyms they retained even after they were well known under their own names. Pseudonyms are also used by authors who write and publish both first-rate and second-rate work and who have the bizarre notion, as we ourselves do, that using a fictitious name for their second-rate work somehow allows them to abrogate their responsibility for having to answer for it.

Reader: Fundamentally, a reader must not be thought of merely as a person who reads; a reader, strictly speaking, is the audience a writer has in mind when he produces his text—the reader as a type of person, say, or even the reader as an ideal, a person who will understand all of his veiled references to the river Styx in Chapter Seven. Obviously, this ideal reader exists solely in the writer's own mind and thus, in a sense, doesn't exist at all.

Rejection slip: An editor's written admission that he or she is obviously much too simple-minded to understand the marketing possibilities for your potboiling memoirs, *Ed Oblonsky: The Cleveland Years*.

Sesquipedalian: Given to using long words. Derives from the Latin, "sesquipedalis," a foot and a half in length. Interestingly, the word, while inherently contemptuous of those who enjoy using long words, is itself a long word. So people who don't know long words but want to say something critically descriptive of those who do probably won't know this word either and therefore can't use it. They must resort to saying something like "Get out of here, you long-word-user." Which hardly turns sesquipedalians flavescent. Quite the contrary, they find such remarks rather diverting, and they like to laugh about them over snails and French bread.

Snack: A hurried or light meal. Writers, as a rule, prefer snacks to full meals. Byron did, as did Auden and thousands of others! Many times writers are too busy creating to be bothered with food, but the body must be fed, so a snack is often the answer. Research done by a Swiss psychologist suggests that by discouraging children from snacking between meals we are inhibiting their artistic inclinations. Her study shows that children who don't snack between meals are more likely to major in business than in comparative literature. Even more disheartening, her study would seem to indicate that children growing up with three round meals a day are sixty-seven percent more likely to become literary agents than they are to become literary.

Somewhat dead: Not to be confused with the undead, the somewhat dead refers to artists and writers who were once very popular and prolific, but who have since drifted off into obscurity, to the point where most people think they are dead. "Isn't he dead?" is a common response when such an artist's name is mentioned. But of course he is not dead; he is just somewhat dead.

Well-crafted: Unpublishable, as in "Dear Mr. Oblonsky: Thank you for sending us *Ed Oblonsky: The Cleveland Years.* Your memoirs, while informative and *well-crafted,* would probably generate little interest outside your immediate family, and for this reason we are returning them to you under separate cover."

Willing suspension of disbelief: Having to do with or pertaining to disbelief and the willing suspension thereof; the willingness to suspend disbelief; the unwillingness not to suspend disbelief; disbelief, its suspension, willed.

WoodyAllenitis: The result of watching too many films by Ingmar Bergman. Usually characterized by a desire to produce more of the same. See Wretched excess.

Wretched excess: That which leads immediately to regret and eventually, one hopes, to wisdom.

Writer's block: A writer's inability to write. Also referred to as being dried up, or stuck in a rut. By definition, writer's block suggests that there is some force between the writer and the work—guilt, say, or self-consciousness, or exhaustion—that is making it impossible for the writer to write. Being dried up is a little different, maybe worse. If you're dried up, you're barren; nothing is coming between you and your work because there is no more work there. You're done for, finished. Sayonara, Mr. Big Shot. Ciao. No more guest spots on the *Today Show* for you! Being stuck in a rut, on the other hand, isn't so bad, because the term implies a temporary situation that can and will be overcome. No one is stuck in a rut forever. But when a writer is stuck, he can't even move a character from one room to another. Scenes just sit still. Tolstoy was stuck in a rut once for two months, and sixteen of his characters died of starvation.

Last night we had this dream. We were alone with our mother in a subway compartment, and the door opened, and there stood . . . Sigmund Freud! And he was HUGE. Our mother turned to us and said, "He's right: it is time for a spanking!" and suddenly the subway car started to rock back and forth, and when it stopped Dr. Freud and Mother were gone, and the cat was on top of the refrigerator, and we cried because we wanted eggs for breakfast, not toast and jam! Our Spanish-speaking maid apologized and flew away, and the cat turned into a bottle of vodka. Then we woke up and smoked a cigar.

—L.T., FEBRUARY 9, 1993

C H A P T E R 36

SOMETIMES A CRACKPOT IS JUST A CRACKPOT.

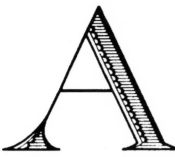T THE END of his fifth
year there, Tolbert quit his job at Cordell, and at this point
we are merely left to recite the string of universities, prep
schools, and community colleges he passed through, remain-
ing at many for just a couple of semesters: Saint Paul's,
Bowling Green, Groton, Simpson Evening College, the
University of North Carolina at Wilmington, Princeton
Country Day School, Greg Lamont's University for the
Betterment of Mankind, the Savannah School of Beauty,
Beaumont Technical Academy and Golf Shop, Rutgers, the
Idaho Outdoor School, the University of Diversity, LSU,
Saint Agnes by the Sea, Beverly Hills High School, and
finally Northern Arizona Community College.

Shortly after the Tolberts arrived in Flagstaff, Dorothea
Tolbert recalls, Leon went to the school's administration
building to inquire about a part-time position in the English
department. There were no positions open, however, part-
time or otherwise. He thanked them and returned to the
motel room where his wife waited, in bed, watching
Jeopardy! and eating Chinese food out of the cartons.

DOROTHEA TOLBERT: *Leon said, "Well, we're all set.
Classes start tomorrow. I'm going to prepare. I want you to go
out apartment hunting." I knew he was lying. Okay, not lying—*

Leon never lied. I knew he was fashioning the world to fit his view of it. After he locked himself in the bathroom to prepare, I called the school and asked them about the part-time English position, and they said, "How odd. You're the second person who's asked about that today. But there is no such position." I thanked them and hung up. I almost confronted Leon about it, but decided not to. I figured he would come back the next day with some cocka-mamie story about how classes were canceled or the school was being quarantined or how there wasn't enough culture in Arizona for him. Sure enough, the next day he returned to the motel look-ing all sad, and I asked him what was wrong, fully expecting to leave town, and he told me: "My classroom is in the basement." My classroom is in the basement. What am I supposed to think about that? Maybe they really hired him. Maybe there was some other position open. But of course there was no other position open. He had simply set up shop in an empty classroom and start-ed to teach. Anyhow, days pass, then weeks, then months, then years. But every time I phone they tell me the same thing: "Lady, there is no position open in the English department. Please stop calling." So I stop, but Leon continues to "teach." We buy a nice house, I get my Reader's Digest subscription, and I even make a couple of friends, though they've asked me not to mention them by name. All this happens, and then I get that call.

CHAPTER 37

Who was it that said, "He who has writ never really dies, for his words live on, be they scorned or mused upon by some future literary soul"? Who said that? Me. I did. So I'm quoting myself. So what.

—L.T., TO HIS WIFE, THE NIGHT
HE WENT TO THE AIRPORT

THE LAST

few weeks of Leon Tolbert's life were marked by frenetic activity, centered almost exclusively around his writing. He worked on new pieces, rewrote old pieces, and spent a great deal of time compiling his work into a form suitable for publication. During his spare moments he made frequent calls to the offices of the *Atlantic Monthly*, prompting its publisher to change the telephone number and install a caller identification system, the first in that venerable magazine's history. This would be Leon Tolbert's sole contribution to the *Atlantic*.

For her part, Dorothea Tolbert was worried. Leon had obviously split the atom of his personality and, in the process, had become something new and different but familiar at the same time. Looking at him was like looking at his image refracted in a broken mirror. He gave her the heebie-jeebies.

Still, she didn't think to consult a doctor or mention his condition, even in passing, to her friends. Her philosophy was that Leon was Leon, always was and always would be, and there was little she could do to change him. She was also watching lots of daytime television and, as she readily admits today, she was "distracted."

The problem was, he seemed happy—content, even. There was no reason he should be, Dorothea felt: his life was in a shambles. His teaching career, such as it was, was over— by now his likeness had been faxed to every institution of higher and lower learning in the land, warning them of his presence; he headed the list of the most unwanted. He had alienated every editor at every magazine and journal in the English-speaking world. The name Tolbert was to literature what the name Oedipus was to family values. He was shut out, blacklisted. He was a literary leper.

And yet he was happy. Why? Did he not know how bad things had become? How far removed from reality *was* he? Apparently quite far indeed. His work proceeded apace. He hummed. He whistled. He talked to himself. He wrote limericks. Dorothea rarely saw him, and when she did, he always mentioned his friends.

"I've got some friends coming in later this week," he said. "I just wanted to let you know. I think you'll like them, no worry on that account. But they may be staying for quite some time."

The week came to an end, and these friends never arrived. Still, Tolbert was not nonplussed.

"I guess they're late," he told her. "Next week, perhaps."

Meanwhile, he wrote, edited, compiled, all in his spare time. From day to day his principles of organization changed. On Monday, he would arrange his writing by date; Tuesday, by the place where he had written it; Wednesday, alphabetically. And so on.

"I envision a grand book," she heard him telling himself. "Like the Bible, but not as dry. Like *Moby Dick* but not as wet. Something right in between."

"Things are moving along!" he told his wife brightly one morning. "My friends will be flying in this Friday."

"From where?" she asked.

"Work!" he said. "Back to work! No rest for the weary!"

Dorothea immersed herself in her soaps. Her current favorite: *One Life to Live*.

When Friday rolled around, Dorothea fully expected it to come and go as uneventfully as the day before. Instead, she found her husband dressing carefully for the first time in months. He had shaved and showered and was wearing a clean, perfectly pressed shirt.

"How do I look?" he asked her, standing before a mirror, knotting his tie.

"You look fine, Leon," she said. "Where are you going?"

"To pick up my pals." Leon went into the bathroom, ran some water, splashed it on his face, and returned, dripping, to the bedroom. "Well, I'm off!" he said.

He looked around the room and at his wife, who sat on the edge of the bed, nearly crying. He took a deep breath. "A hug?" he said.

"You'll drive carefully?" she asked him.

"Don't worry," he said. "I'll be fine. Just zip to the airport and zip back." And he was gone.

An hour later Dorothea received a phone call from the airport. Eluding security, her husband had inexplicably wandered onto an active runway, directly into the path of Flight 601 from Miami.

Death for Leon Tolbert was immediate and obliterating.

POSTSCRIPT

Leon Tolbert's memorial service was a lonely one. His wife was there, as were his parents, Edwin and Stella, now well into their nineties and completely senile: they had no idea what they were doing there. Edwin kept asking for a glass of water, and Stella told Dorothea: "I've never liked these parties, have you?" Dorothea had hoped that one or two of Leon's students might show up, but none did, and when it was over, she walked off into the rain alone.[1]

Leon Tolbert lived a life, and then he died; no words can fully explain how or why. Who Tolbert was and the reasons behind the choices he made are perhaps only sketchily represented here, but a man who lives by the sword dies by the sword; and a man who lives by the word must be content for complete strangers to walk into his life, look through his most personal effects, read his most intimate diaries, even poke through his underwear drawer.[2] This, at any rate, is what we have done. And what are we left with? A tale that ends in one man's desperate attempt to be united with those writers he loved most. And questions. We are left with lots of questions, some of which can never be answered. It is only when we stop asking them, however, that Leon Tolbert's life will cease to matter.

---

1. *It wasn't really raining. The widow Tolbert liked the image and insisted we stick it there. The editors apologize.*

2. *Every biographer does this. We swear.*